D0618416

THE WAY PEOPLE LIVE

Life on the American Frontier

Titles in The Way People Live series include:

THE WAY
PEOPLE
LIVE

Life on the American Frontier

by Stuart A. Kallen

Lucent Books, P.O. Box 289011, San Diego, CA 92198-9011

HOUSTON PUBLIC LIBRARY

RO1118 18801

Library of Congress Cataloging-in-Publication Data

Kallen, Stuart A., 1955–
    Life on the American frontier / by Stuart A. Kallen.
        p.   cm. — (The way people live)
    Includes bibliographical references and index.
    Summary: Discusses how people on the American frontier lived,
including trailblazers, fur trappers, mountain men, Native Americans,
miners, cowboys, and pioneers.
    ISBN 1-56006-366-1 (lib. bdg. : alk. paper)
    1. Frontier and pioneer life—West (U.S.)—Juvenile literature.   2. West
(U.S.)—Social conditions—Juvenile literature.   3. West (U.S.)—Social life
and customs—Juvenile literature.   [1. Frontier and pioneer life—West
(U.S.)   2. West (U.S.)—Social life and customs.]   I. Title.   II. Series.
F596.A386   1999
978—dc21   98-19328
                                                                                      CIP
                                                                                      AC

Copyright 1999 by Lucent Books, Inc., P.O. Box 289011, San Diego, California
92198-9011

No part of this book may be reproduced or used in any other form or by any
other means, electrical, mechanical, or otherwise, including, but not limited to,
photocopy, recording, or any information storage and retrieval system, without
prior written permission from the publisher.

Printed in the U.S.A.

Contents

Discovering the Humanity in Us All

Books in The Way People Live series focus on groups of people in a wide variety of circumstances, settings, and time periods. Some books focus on different cultural groups, others, on people in a particular historical time period, while others cover people involved in a specific event. Each book emphasizes the daily routines, personal and historical struggles, and achievements of people from all walks of life.

To really understand any culture, it is necessary to strip the mind of the common notions we hold about groups of people. These stereotypes are the archenemies of learning. It does not even matter whether the stereotypes are positive or negative; they are confining and tight. Removing them is a challenge that's not easily met, as anyone who has ever tried it will admit. Ideas that do not fit into the templates we create are unwelcome visitors—ones we would prefer remain quietly in a corner or forgotten room.

The cowboy of the Old West is a good example of such confining roles. The cowboy was courageous, yet soft-spoken. His time (it is always a he, in our template) was spent alternatively saving a rancher's daughter from certain death on a runaway stagecoach, or shooting it out with rustlers. At times, of course, he was likely to get a little crazy in town after a trail drive, but for the most part, he was the epitome of inner strength. It is disconcerting to find out that the cowboy is human, even a bit childish. Can it really be true that cowboys would line up to help the cook on the trail drive grind coffee, just hoping he would give them a little stick of peppermint candy that came with the coffee shipment? The idea of tough cowboys vying with one another to help "Coosie" (as they called their cooks) for a bit of candy seems silly and out of place.

So is the vision of Eskimos playing video games and watching MTV, living in prefab housing in the Arctic. It just does not fit with what "Eskimo" means. We are far more comfortable with snow igloos and whale blubber, harpoons and kayaks.

Although the cultures dealt with in Lucent's The Way People Live series are often historically and socially well known, the emphasis is on the personal aspects of life. Groups of people, while unquestionably affected by their politics and their governmental structures, are more than those institutions. How do people in a particular time and place educate their children? What do they eat? And how do they build their houses? What kinds of work do they do? What kinds of games do they enjoy? The answers to these questions bring these cultures to life. People's lives are revealed in the particulars and only by knowing the particulars can we understand these cultures' will to survive and their moments of weakness and greatness.

This is not to say that understanding politics does not help to understand a culture. There is no question that the Warsaw ghetto, for example, was a culture that was brought about by the politics and social ideas of Adolf

Hitler and the Third Reich. But the Jews who were crowded together in the ghetto cannot be understood by the Reich's politics. Their life was a day-to-day battle for existence, and the creativity and methods they used to prolong their lives is a vital story of human perseverance that would be denied by focusing only on the institutions of Hitler's Germany. Knowing that children as young as five or six outwitted Nazi guards on a daily basis, that Jewish policemen helped the Germans control the ghetto, that children attended secret schools in the ghetto and even earned diplomas—these are the things that reveal the fabric of life, that can inspire, intrigue, and amaze.

Books in The Way People Live series allow both the casual reader and the student to see humans as victims, heroes, and onlookers. And although humans act in ways that can fill us with feelings of sorrow and revulsion, it is important to remember that "hero," "predator," and "victim" are dangerous terms. Heaping undue pity or praise on people reduces them to objects, and strips them of their humanity.

Seeing the Jews of Warsaw only as victims is to deny their humanity. Seeing them only as they appear in surviving photos, staring at the camera with infinite sadness, is limiting, both to them and to those who want to understand them. To an object of pity, the only appropriate response becomes "Those poor creatures!" and that reduces both the quality of their struggle and the depth of their despair. No one is served by such two-dimensional views of people and their cultures.

With this in mind, The Way People Live series strives to flesh out the traditional, two-dimensional views of people in various cultures and historical circumstances. Using a wide variety of primary quotations—the words not only of the politicians and government leaders, but of the real people whose lives are being examined—each book in the series attempts to show an honest and complete picture of a culture removed from our own by time or space.

By examining cultures in this way, the reader will notice not only the glaring differences from his or her own culture, but also will be struck by the similarities. For indeed, people share common needs—warmth, good company, stability, and affirmation from others. Ultimately, seeing how people really live, or have lived, can only enrich our understanding of ourselves.

The Ever-Moving Frontier

For more than four hundred years, the frontier regions of America were an ever-shifting area that spanned an entire continent. From the tidewater regions of New England to the California coast, the American frontier moved steadily west for more than a dozen generations.

Because the regions kept changing, the American frontier is defined more by its people than its actual geographic boundaries. The story of the American frontier may best be seen through the eyes of European American and African American people who settled the land—and the Native Americans who lost their land in the process. Pioneers were all sorts of people—rich, poor, ex-slaves, saints, and sinners. But they seemed to have one idea in common: that a better world lay over the next horizon. So they pushed and pushed westward until the frontier was conquered and a modern nation rose from its bounty.

Where Was the Frontier?

Great Britain ruled the eastern seaboard of America from the early 1600s until the late 1700s. In 1776 America declared independence, went to war with Britain, and threw off the yoke of British rule. After the American Revolution the boundaries of the new United States doubled in size. From the Great Lakes in the North to the Gulf of Mexico in the South, the United States stretched from the eastern seaboard to the Mississippi River. (The exception was Florida, which would be added later.)

The new lands would soon be filled by people escaping hardships in Europe. About 250,000 poor Germans left behind wars, persecution, and bad harvests. A quarter million Scotch-Irish ran from high rents and poor land in Scotland and northern England. The human tide spread into Pennsylvania. It turned north into New England and south down to the Appalachian Mountains and into the Carolinas.

The population growth was stupendous. In 1790 only 4,300 white settlers lived in the Ohio territories. By 1800 that number had grown to 45,000. In that same year, over 700,000 white settlers lived west of the Appalachian Mountains, where there had been none twenty years earlier.

The Appalachian Frontier

In the late eighteenth century, the entire North American continent from the Atlantic to the Mississippi was one vast forest broken by an occasional prairie, lake, river, or swamp. Huge spruce, hemlock, and fir trees covered the higher peaks of northern New England all the way down to Tennessee. Oaks and chestnuts flourished from New Jersey through Pennsylvania to northern Virginia. Pines and oaks dominated the South. The forests were filled with deer, squirrels, bears, wildcats, panthers, snakes, and wolves.

After the Revolution, restless Americans and European immigrants began streaming into the mountains of Kentucky, Tennessee, Pennsylvania, Virginia, the Carolinas, and Ohio. And they did so in defiance of the Native Americans who roamed those vast hunting grounds.

The U.S. government controlled the lands of this immense frontier. Congress passed a law called the Ordinance of 1785 that appointed surveyors in each state. The surveyors divided the territory into townships six miles square. The townships were divided into lots of 640 acres, or one square mile. These plots in turn were sold to the public at a minimum price of $1 an acre.

In 1787 Congress passed the Northwest Ordinance, which created a district called the Northwest Territory. The ordinance described ways that self-government was to be established on the American frontier. When a territory's population reached sixty thousand people, it could frame its own constitution and become a state. In 1791, Vermont became the first post-Revolution state admitted to the Union. Kentucky became a state in 1792, Tennessee in 1796. The first state in the Northwest Territory was Ohio, admitted to the Union in

Appalachian Life

The backwoodsmen and women had no use for the rules and regulations of East Coast society. They hacked out clearings with their axes and built log cabins to live in. Their rifles and shotguns provided them with clothing and food. When game got scarce or neighbors too close, they would pick up and move deeper into the wilderness. Historian

Thomas Clark writes about the lonely life in the deep woods of the Appalachian Mountains in his book *The Rampaging Frontier.*

"Distances were great, neighborhoods were scattered, but once the mountains were crossed, denizens of the backwoods learned to get along without company. A generation of people came into existence to whom the faintest tinkling of a stranger's cowbell or the barking of his dog caused life to become oppressive, and it was time 'to be gittin' on.'"

A typical backwoods couple and their roughly constructed home.

1803. When a territory became a state it attracted even more pioneers to the area.

Kentucky boasted a quarter million people by 1800. There were about half that many in Tennessee. By 1810 over 200,000 crowded into Ohio. The West began changing. The sons of wealthy planters moved to Kentucky with slaves and heavy furniture. They cleared great tracts of forest and planted tobacco. Doctors, lawyers, and merchants came over the hills to seek a new life in Louisville, Lexington, Knoxville, and Fort Washington (now Cincinnati). The Appalachian areas began to fill up. But a whole new world was about to open up west of the Mississippi River.

The Louisiana Purchase and Texas

By 1803 the Appalachian frontier was quickly filling up with pioneers. That year, President Thomas Jefferson purchased the Louisiana Territory from France for $15 million. Jefferson's actions made him a national hero. But his political enemies called the purchase "the wildest chimera of a moonstruck brain."[1] They argued that Jefferson paid $15 million for land he knew nothing about.

Jefferson's opponents were right. The treaty of purchase specified an area of 909,130 square miles. But the final survey turned up only 800,000 square miles. Jefferson knew the purchase extended west to the Continental Divide—but no one knew where that was either. The president intended to find out. In the spring of 1804, Jefferson sent Meriwether Lewis, William Clark, and a thirty-man team of trailblazers to explore the lands.

After Lewis and Clark mapped out the Louisiana Territory, Americans began moving into the area. By the 1820s they were spilling into the Mexican territory of Texas. The Americans ignored Mexico's right of ownership and staked out claims for ranches and farms. By 1830 Texas was occupied by a majority of American settlers. Within five years, they formed their own government within Texas.

Lewis and Clark journeyed across the Louisiana Purchase, encountering Native American tribes that already lived on the new American frontier.

In 1836 the Texas Americans declared independence from Mexico. Sam Houston was named commander-in-chief of the army. After a brief battle with the Mexican army, Texas became an independent country free of Mexican rule. On December 29, 1845, Texas became the twenty-eighth state to join the Union.

Manifest Destiny

In the 1840s, many Americans became obsessed with the region west of the Mississippi. The area was thought of as a wilderness that could be turned into a home to common people—a place where a family could carve out a farm, raise a family, or start a business.

The movement to develop the West was known as Manifest Destiny. At the heart of Manifest Destiny was the belief that America should be "civilized" from sea to shining sea. This was somehow in keeping with a higher power—nature, history, or God. The movement took on the feel of a crusade. It became a person's patriotic duty to pull up stakes and move west. The U.S. senator from Missouri, Thomas Hart Benton, was one of the main believers in Manifest Destiny. He summed up its meaning with one flowery sentence: "In a few years time, the Rocky Mountains will be passed and the 'children of Adam' will have completed the circumambulation of the globe by marching west until they arrive at the Pacific Ocean."[2]

To aid Manifest Destiny, the U.S. army formed the Corps of Topographical Engineers in 1838. This organization was made up of surveyors and mapmakers who had graduated near the top of their class at West Point. Their job was to make maps for the army. But they wound up leading an army of pioneers across the entire continent to the Pacific.

Senator Thomas Hart Benton believed that Americans were destined to move west and settle the land that was now part of the expanding nation.

Between 1840 and 1860 the Topographical Corps mapped out postal and wagon-train routes across the West. They published atlases to help make the West accessible to settlers. The corps also mapped out the current boundaries of the United States; Britain still laid claim to the Oregon Territory and the Spanish claimed California and New Mexico.

Filling in the Borders

In 1846 the United States went to war with Mexico. At issue were the California and New Mexico Territories. After a short war, and a humiliating Mexican defeat, the Rio Grande became the new border between Mexico and the United States. The United States agreed to pay Mexico $15 million for all of California, New Mexico, and Arizona.

While American soldiers were fighting Mexico, the United States was trying to secure title to the Oregon Territory in the Pacific

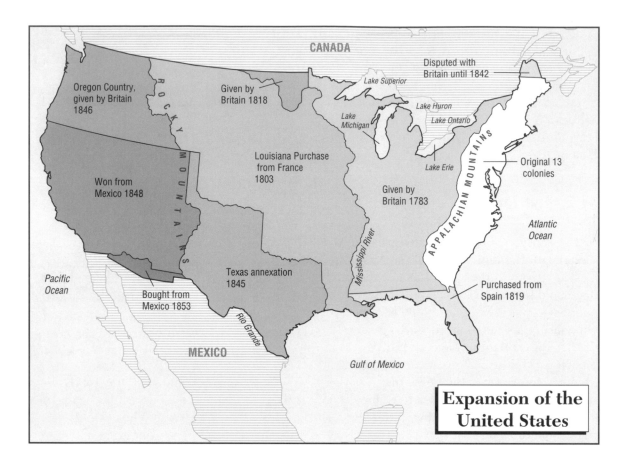

CANADA

Oregon Country, given by Britain 1846

Given by Britain 1818

Disputed with Britain until 1842

Lake Superior

Lake Huron

Lake Michigan

Lake Ontario

ROCKY MOUNTAINS

Louisiana Purchase from France 1803

Won from Mexico 1848

APPALACHIAN MOUNTAINS

Original 13 colonies

Lake Erie

Given by Britain 1783

Atlantic Ocean

Mississippi River

Pacific Ocean

Texas annexation 1845

Bought from Mexico 1853

Rio Grande

Purchased from Spain 1819

MEXICO

Gulf of Mexico

Expansion of the United States

Northwest. The land had been jointly owned by the United States and Britain since 1818. In 1843 four thousand Americans migrated into the Oregon Territory via the Oregon Trail that ran from Kansas City to modern-day Portland.

In 1846 the United States signed a treaty with Britain setting the northern border of the United States at the forty-ninth parallel. This added the modern states of Oregon, Washington, and Idaho. After a small sliver of land was bought along the Rio Grande in Arizona in 1853, the U.S. borders became what they are today.

The Big Country

Between 1800 and 1880 the population of the United States grew from 5 million to over 50 million. By the 1880s, the last veil had been stripped from the mystery of the West. In the short span of eighty years the frontier had been walked, ridden, surveyed, photographed, painted, and written about. In the course of one human lifetime, America was mapped to its furthest corners. But if the mystery faded, the awesome proportions of the West still fired the imaginations of pioneers.

The Trailblazers

Rivers great and small were the highways for early pioneers moving west. Where the rivers narrowed, backwoods people followed trails like the Warrior's Path, a single-file footpath worn smooth by centuries of Native American travel. After a few hardy souls blazed a trail, scattered settlements soon followed.

In the mid-eighteenth century, the eastern slopes of the Appalachian Mountains were explored by hundreds of hunters and

The Cumberland Gap allowed homesteaders easy access to the land beyond the Appalachian Mountains.

scouts. These men searched through the dense forests and steep mountains for an easy pass to the Western frontier. It was finally found in 1750 by an English doctor who had gone west as an agent for a Virginia land company. Thomas Walker found a gap in the mountains at 1,665 feet above sea level. The natural gap was on the border of the modern states of Kentucky, Tennessee, and Virginia. Native Americans had beaten it down for decades. From there a great system of trails branched out to the south and west. Walker named the pass after the duke of Cumberland and returned home. The Cumberland Gap would remain the most important pass to the West for more than a century.

The Wilderness Road later funneled through the Cumberland Gap and across Kentucky. The hills of Tennessee were penetrated by the Old Walton Road. And in 1796, Congress ordered Zane's Trace to be cut across the Ohio River basin. These passages would lure many trailblazers to explore what lay on the other sides of these daunting natural boundaries.

Daniel Boone, the Trailblazer

Daniel Boone was one of the earliest Americans to venture into the unknown lands. By trade, Boone was a land speculator, blacksmith, tavern keeper, and collector of ginseng root, which he shipped to China. But these undertakings were secondary to his fame as a

Believing there was opportunity and wealth in the Kentucky wilderness, Daniel Boone headed a party of trailblazers to open the region to settlers.

man of the forest. Boone was one of the earliest "long hunters" who crossed the Appalachians in the 1760s. Sometimes he would roam for up to two years. By the time he died in 1818, Boone, the trailblazer, was one of the most famous Americans.

Born in Pennsylvania in 1736, Boone moved to North Carolina's western frontier in 1750. This was wild country. Boone bragged that he could shoot a dozen deer before noon. With an eye for profit, he would carry their hides by packhorse to sell in market towns. Boone later married and had ten children. He farmed a bit in the spring and summer, then disappeared—to hunt in the autumn and trap beaver in the winter through the "vast solicitudes of the Appalachian wilderness."[3]

Boone sold the pelts of the animals he hunted for profit. In 1769 he assembled horses and pack animals, kettles, traps, salt, lead, gunpowder, spare blankets, rum, and rations. He also brought for the expedition extra hunters and several "camp keepers" who would cook, prepare hides, and kill game if necessary.

Boone and his party pushed into the Kentucky wilderness, where they explored eight thousand square miles of untouched woodlands and rolling, grassy hills. After being kidnapped by and escaping from the Shawnee tribe, Boone wandered alone through the "Kaintuck" frontier. Without "bread, salt, sugar, horse, or dog, he began a single-handed investigation of western Kentucky in which he learned the land as thoroughly as the Indians."[4] When he returned to civilization in 1771, he was convinced that the bluegrass country would make him his fortune.

Boone set out again in 1775, this time with thirty armed axmen. They started from eastern Tennessee to clear a continuous road west through the narrow Cumberland Gap. The woodsmen went through the gap, following Indian trails and bison trails. They rolled away rocks, hacked down forest and brush, and posted guide marks at difficult sites. In fourteen days they hacked a packhorse road over the Cumberland Gap and then west along the ancient Warrior's Path. Before long, pioneers followed, settling the rudimentary villages of Boonesborough, Harrodsburg, and Logan's Station.

The work of Boone and his men became known as the Wilderness Road. It was three hundred miles long and ended at the Ohio River near Louisville. Boone's exhausting trailblazing feat was immortalized in books, ballads, and tall tales. These, in turn, inspired more than a hundred thousand people to tramp into the Tennessee and Kentucky Territories during the next fifteen years.

By 1795 the road was graded for wagons. Within another twenty-five years, the population of the United States doubled to 10 million. The overflow of Americans, along with the new arrivals, made the Wilderness Road the main southern highway to the West.

Lewis and Clark's Corps of Discovery

By the beginning of the nineteenth century, the Appalachian Mountains were filling up with thousands of pioneers. But there were new horizons to explore even further west on the American continent. In 1803 the Louisiana Purchase added 800,000 square miles of virgin wilderness to the United States west of the Mississippi River. By the time the land transfer from France was complete in 1804, Thomas Jefferson's secretary, Meriwether Lewis, had assembled a team of thirty men called the Corps of Discovery. With his co-commander William Clark, the men left to find a route to the Pacific on March 9, 1804.

The Joy of Frontier Living

Although Appalachian pioneers faced many hardships, there was great reward thought to be found in their lifestyles. Victor Barringer, a writer in early Tennessee, romanticized the early frontier society in Parke Rouse Jr.'s *The Great Wagon Road*. This sort of prose attracted thousands of pioneers when it was read in the newspapers of the East.

"The early occupants of log cabins were among the most happy of mankind. Exercise and excitement gave them health; they were practically equal; common danger made them mutually dependent; brilliant hopes of future wealth and distinction led them on; and as there was ample room for all, and as each newcomer increased individual and general security, there was little room for that envy, jealousy, and hatred which constitute a large portion of human misery in older societies.

Never were the story, the song and the laugh better enjoyed than upon the hewed blocks, or puncheon [barrel] stools, around the roaring log fire of the early western settler."

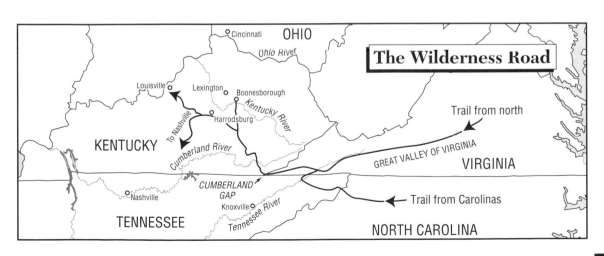

The Wilderness Road

The Corps of Discovery consisted of nine young men from Kentucky, fourteen soldiers from the U.S. army who volunteered their services, two French watermen, an interpreter, a hunter, and Clark's black servant, York. In addition, the party enlisted seven soldiers and nine watermen to accompany them as far as North Dakota to repel expected attacks by Native Americans.

The party embarked on board three boats. Two horses were led along the banks of the river for the purposes of hunting. For the next two years, four months, and ten days the Corps of Discovery was beyond the edge of the world known to white America. They rowed, paddled, trudged, and rode horseback from Missouri to the Pacific Ocean.

Before they left, Jefferson gave them a written statement of purpose: "The object of your mission is to explore the Missouri River, & such principal stream of it, as, by it's course & communication with the waters of the Pacific Ocean . . . may offer the most direct and practical water communication across this continent for the purposes of commerce."[5]

On May 14 the expedition started up the Missouri River. They had not gone far when they found much to marvel at, as Lewis described.

> This senery already rich peleasing and beatiful was still farther hightened by immensce herds of Buffaloe, deer Elk, and Antelopes which we saw in every direction. . . . The Buffaloe Elk and Antelope are so gentle that we pass near them . . . without appearing to excite any alarm among them. They frequently approach us more nearly to discover who we are.[6]

Not all was wonderment and excitement, however. They complained constantly of clouds of gnats, blood-sucking "Musquiters," and dangerous water hazards in the Missouri.

By the autumn of 1804, the party reached the mouth of the Knife River in modern-day North Dakota, where they decided to spend the winter among the Mandan Indians. The corps erected a sturdy fort. That winter, temperatures fell to forty-five degrees below zero. Lewis noted that it was so cold that the expedition's liquor that had been left outside froze solid in fifteen minutes.

During their five-month stopover, Clark found a chief named Big White who knew the terrain far ahead. The expedition leader spent hours translating the chief's crude maps, which were drawn in the sand. While wintering with the Mandan, Lewis recruited a French-Canadian man named Toussaint Charbonneau to join the expedition. Charbonneau's wife was a Shoshone named Sacajawea. (Lewis

William Clark was co-commander of the Corps of Discovery, a military expedition that attempted to find an all-water route to the Pacific Ocean.

Lewis and Clark met several Indian tribes along their journey. Some of the native people aided the explorers either by accompanying the expedition or by describing what lay ahead.

and Clark wrote of her as "the Indian woman" because they could not spell her name.) Sacajawea had been kidnapped by the Mandan tribe at age eleven and sold to Charbonneau as a slave. Now sixteen and very pregnant, Sacajawea wanted to join the expedition to get back to the Shoshone people in the West. Before they left, she gave birth to a son.

Life in the Corps of Discovery

Life in the Corps of Discovery was a mixture of wonder and hardship. When Lewis came upon the Rockies in Montana, he wrote: "These points of the Rocky Mountains were covered with snow and the sun shone on it in such a manner as to give me the most plain and satisfactory view. While I viewed these mountains I felt a secret pleasure." But at the same time, the beautiful mountains posed a huge barrier to the corps. "But when I reflected on the difficulties which this snowey

barrier would throw in my way to the Pacific, and the sufferings and hardships of myself and party in thim [them], it counterballanced the joy I had felt in the first moments in which I gazed on them."[7]

Before they could even get to the mountains, the corps came across the Great Falls of the Missouri. The roaring torrent was three hundred yards wide and eighty feet high. The portage around the falls stretched eighteen miles. The rough terrain was so overgrown with spiky cactus that the men were tormented through their double-soled moccasins. (Blistered, bruised, and bloodied feet were a common complaint among the men in the corps, and Lewis often made mention of the problem.) To move the heavy equipment, the men set about hewing primitive cart wheels from a cottonwood tree. For the next twenty-four days, the men used these wheels to inch their canoes and baggage around the waterfall.

All this work was done in a continual plague of cold weather and rain. This can be

After exploring the Louisiana Territory for three months, Lewis and Clark met up with the first of many Native Americans who lived in the area. Meriwether Lewis's speech, printed in *The Journals of Lewis and Clark*, helped set the pattern of official U.S. policy toward Indians in the West.

"Children. The great chief of the Seventeen great nations (states) of America, impelled by his parental regard for his newly adopted children on the troubled waters, has sent us out to clear the road. . . . [He] has commanded us his war chiefs to undertake this long journey. . . . You are to live in peace with all white men, for they are his children; neither wage war against the red men, your neighbors, for they are equally his children. Injure not the person of any traders who may come among you. Do these things your father advises and be happy. Avoid the council of bad birds; turn on your heel from them . . . lest by one false step you should bring upon your nation the displeasure of your great father . . . who could consume you as the fire consumes the grass of the plains."

Lewis was a great deal more gracious than those who followed him, but the message to the natives was still clear: You are children to us. Be obedient or we will destroy you. Over the next ninety years, those who followed Lewis and Clark did indeed consume the natives as the fire consumed the grass.

Meriwether Lewis

seen on page after page of Lewis's diary. At different times he wrote: "rained and blew hard last night, some hard Thunder with a high wind from the Southeast," "rained last night as usial and the greater part of this day," "Fog so thick this morning could not see a man 50 steps off."[8]

Bugs were another torture. As Lewis described,

The fleas which annoyed us have taken such a possession of our clothes, that we are obliged to have a regular search every day through our blankets. These animals are indeed so numerous, that they are almost a calamity to the Indians of this Country. Every Indian is constantly attended by multitudes of them, and no one comes into our houses without leaving behind him swarms of these tormenting insects.[9]

Finding food was a constant source of drudgery among the men. Sometimes they had great luck finding fish, geese, ducks, and deer to eat. Other times they were forced to near starvation as their hunters searched far and wide for something to eat. While crossing the Rockies, Lewis wrote, "This morning I arrose very early and hungary as a wolf. I had nothing yesterday except one scant meal of the dried cakes of berries which did not appear to satisfy my appetite as they appeared to do those of my Indian friends. I found that we had only about two pounds of flour remaining." [10]

Though suffering all sorts of hardships, Lewis and Clark ran the corps with strict military discipline. Early on, a man named Moses Reed deserted the group. He was captured by other corpsmen, given a quick trial, and subjected to twenty-five lashes with a whip. Later, a man who was not performing his duties properly was lashed seventy-five times and discharged from the expedition, which was witnessed by the Native Americans. Clark wrote: "The punishment of this day allrmed. the Indian Chief verry much, he cried aloud." [11]

One of the most unusual facets of the journey was that Sacajawea was allowed to lead the corps as they neared the source of the Missouri. She recognized landmarks and helped guide the men up into the mountains. Thanks to her, the Shoshones provided the corps with horses. When the expedition set out again, in August, Sacajawea chose to go with them. She, her husband, and her infant son would stay with the party until they returned to North Dakota a year later.

The Rumbling Pacific and Back to Civilization

Coming down the western face of the Rockies, the corps was forced to abandon their canoes. They trekked down the ribbed ledges, torrential creeks, and steep slopes on Shoshone horses. The wild game seemed to have vanished as the men followed the Columbia River through present-day Idaho and Oregon. The corps eked out meager meals with a small stock of horse meat, an occasional grouse, dogs, coyote, and even a crow. By then, many of the men had dysentery, as Clark wrote: "Lax & heaviness at the stomack. Capt. Lewis

Sacajawea, the native wife of one of the expedition's guides, led the party through the lands she remembered from her childhood.

verry sick, scercely able to ride on a jentle horse. Several men So unwell that they were Compelled to lie on the Side of the road for Sometime. Our men nearly all Complaining of their bowels." [12]

Quite suddenly on November 7, 1805, the party heard the rumble of the Pacific Ocean. Clark described the event: "Great joy in camp we are in view of the Ocian, this great Pacific Octean which we been so long anxious to See. and the roreing or noise made by the waves brakeing on the rockey Shores (as I suppose) may be heard distinctly." [13]

By December the corps was camping on the south bank of the Columbia River, near its mouth. By January the group had hewed a stockade and winter quarters named Fort Clatsop. After a soggy winter of constant rain, the corps readied to go home. They broke camp on March 23, 1806.

The journey back was somewhat easier. On September 20, 1806, the Corps of Discovery passed a French settlers' village. It was the first sign of white civilization they had seen in more than two and a half years. Clark wrote, "We saw some cows on the bank which was a joyfull Sight to the party and caused a Shout to be raised for joy." [14]

Most people had given up hope on Lewis and Clark. News of their return spread quickly. Newspapers across the land rushed summaries of their journey into print. The expedition had lost only one man. With strength, endurance, and discipline, they had opened up a route to half a continent. Moreover, the corps had gone into the unknown and proven that North America was twice the size previously believed.

Lewis and Clark kept detailed notes throughout their journey of 7,689 punishing

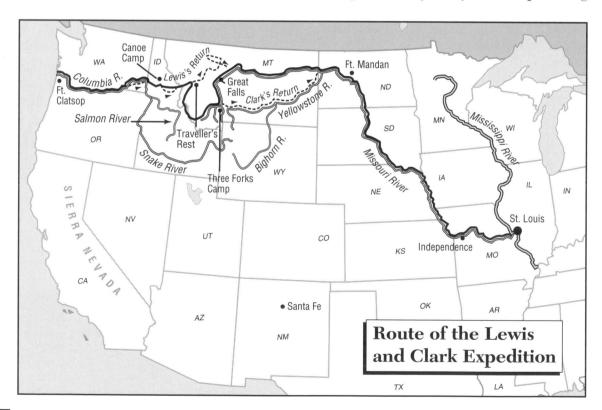

Route of the Lewis and Clark Expedition

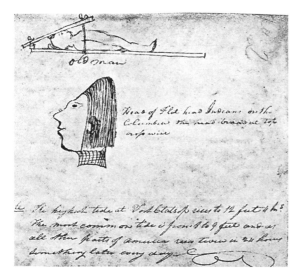

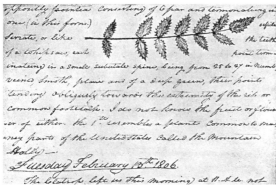

Lewis and Clark and other members of their expedition kept journals that described the people, plants, and animals they encountered on the way. These proved valuable to scientists back East.

miles through trackless country. They made maps and filled over a dozen notebooks. The expedition also collected hundreds of plant and animal specimens, many of them new to the scientific world.

The Mountain Men Open the Rockies to California

In 1806, en route back to civilization, Lewis and Clark encountered two men heading up the Missouri River to trap beaver in Yellowstone country. These rugged trailblazers were already heading off into the unknown country that Lewis and Clark had not yet put on the map.

The second wave of Western exploration was led by a ragtag bunch of tough fur trappers who were called mountain men. These men traveled through the Rocky Mountains looking for beaver and other valuable pelts. The mountain men came upon the steaming geysers, towering snow-capped mountains, and great salt lakes. They tangled with grizzly bears and mountain lions and froze beneath snows that reached to the treetops.

When mountain men reported the fantastic sights they had seen, few believed them. "They said I was the damnedest liar ever lived," complained Jim Bridger, one of the boldest mountain men. "That's what a man gets for telling the truth." [15]

In 1833 one of the toughest mountain men was thirty-four-year-old Joseph Walker. He had long hair, a full beard, and wore clothing made by Native Americans. Walker helped survey the Santa Fe Trail that ran from Independence, Missouri, to Santa Fe, New Mexico. And he led a one-hundred-man party of trappers through the rough canyons of the Snake and Salmon Rivers in Idaho.

Walker assembled a party of forty men to blaze an overland trail to California. In 1833 the vast areas of modern Utah, Arizona, Nevada, and eastern California were virtually unexplored. The Spaniards lived along the coast of California, but few white people—if any—had ever attempted to cross the Sierra Nevada.

With tales of warm winter weather, mission wineries, and an endless ocean shore, Walker did not have a hard time recruiting men to go on his expedition. Each man in the Walker team began his mission with four horses and sixty pounds of dried and jerked meat.

Jim Bridger was one of the first mountain men to investigate the Rocky Mountains.

The Walker Party and the Native Americans

Walker followed the example set by Lewis and Clark. Whenever he encountered local Native Americans, he interrogated them about the nature of the country that lay ahead and the best possible routes through the wilderness. In this manner, the Walker party crossed the harsh, desolate lands of northern Utah and Nevada.

When the trailblazers arrived in western Nevada, they came across a band of Paiute Indians. Although numerous, they were very thin and poor. They subsisted in a Stone Age manner by grubbing up roots, beetles, and lizards. The Paiutes were amazed at the metal tools of the Walker expedition and were particularly fascinated by the beaver traps, of which they stole a few.

Later, while some of the explorers were out hunting, they came across a few Paiutes. Zenas Leonard, a member of the party who later wrote a book, described what happened:

So eager were [the Paiutes] to possess our traps that we were forced to quit trapping in this vicinity. The great annoyance we sustained in this respect greatly displeased some of the men, and they were for taking vengeance before we left the country—but this was not the disposition of Captain Walker. These discontents being out hunting one day, fell in with a few Indians, two or three of whom they killed, and returned to camp, not daring to let the Captain know it. The next day while hunting, they repeated the same violation—but this time not so successful, for the Captain found it out, and immediately took measures for its effectual suppression.[16]

Although Walker raged at the men for needlessly provoking the natives, the damage was done. The Paiutes surrounded the forty mountain men, their numbers increasing ominously until they totaled eight hundred. Never before having seen guns, the Paiutes were not frightened by the white men's show of arms. Even a shooting exhibition did not impress the natives. Finally the mountain men attacked the Paiutes, killing thirty-nine. At that point the threat to the mountain men was over. But the expedition's largest barrier lay ahead.

Gazing Down on Yosemite

Walking west in Nevada the Walker party came to the unbroken mass of the Sierra Nevada.

The granite wall stretched north-south for four hundred miles and reached heights of fourteen thousand feet. The men pressed on, following rivers and creeks. Leonard wrote:

> As we advanced, sometimes we would encounter prodigious quantities of snow. A certain portion of the men would be appointed to go forward and break the road, to enable our horses to get through; and if any of the horses would get swamped, these same men were to get them out. In this tedious and tiresome manner, we spent the whole day without going more than eight or ten miles.[17]

After three weeks of hunger and punishing work crossing the Sierra Nevada, the Walker party stood upon a mountain peak and gazed down at the beautiful Yosemite Valley below. It had never before been seen by a white man.

The floor of the Yosemite Valley was more than seven miles long. It was studded with granite monoliths that rose from the valley for more than fifteen hundred feet. One night the men in the Walker party saw a meteor shower. "This was a mystery to some of the men," Leonard wrote, "but after an explanation from Captain Walker they were satisfied that no danger need be apprehended from the falling of the stars."[18]

Walker's party continued on in the warm California sun. There they were warmly greeted by the Mexican people who lived there. After three months of eating, drinking, and sport, Walker headed back east. In 1834

Suffering Along the Trail

Most trailblazers were ordinary men who undertook extraordinary adventures. One mountain man who wrote down his experiences was Zenas Leonard. In the fall of 1831, Leonard and seventeen other men were trapped in the deep snows of a canyon on the Laramie River. The men tried to walk eight hundred miles through the mountains to Santa Fe, although none was certain of the city's location. In his autobiography, *The Adventures of Zenas Leonard,* the author wrote:

"Here we are in the desolate wilderness uninhabited by even the hardy savage or beast—surrounded on either side by huge mountains of snow, without one mouthful to eat save a few beaver skins—our eyes almost destroyed by piercing wind, and our bodies at times almost buried by the flakes of snow, which were driven before it. Oh! How heartily I wished myself home."

The men decided to make snowshoes and continue walking.

"This appeared to present to us the only means of escape from starvation and death. After gathering up everything of leather kind that could be found, we got to making snowshoes. . . . But what were we to subsist upon while crossing the mountain was a painful question that agitated every bosom and employed every tongue in company. Provision, we had none of any description; having eaten everything we had that could be eaten . . . and, after having fasted several days, to attempt to travel the distance of the valley without anything to eat, appeared almost worse than useless."

Leonard survived the ordeal to later accompany Captain Joseph Walker over the Sierra Nevada, blazing the first overland route to northern California.

The passage across the Sierra Nevada was difficult, but the sight of the Yosemite Valley on the other side was spectacular.

he found a low pass over the Sierras at fifty-two hundred feet. Within a few years, Walker Pass would become the main point of entry for emigrants bound for California.

Joseph Walker's life was possibly the best illustration of American frontier exploration. He headed across the Mississippi when the West was still a blank place on the map. As a mountain man, he helped fill in the blanks. As a believer in Manifest Destiny, he fought to make California part of the United States. As a guide, he brought settlers to the Pacific shores. Perhaps his epitaph best sums up frontier exploration in the nineteenth century.

Joseph Walker
Born in Roan County, Tennessee.
December 13, 1798.
Emigrated to Missouri, 1819.
To New Mexico, 1820.
Rocky Mountains, 1832.
California, 1833.
Camped at Yosemite,
November 13, 1833.[19]

Fur Trappers and Mountain Men

After Lewis and Clark opened the frontier, thousands of people—mostly men—poured into the far West. Many made their living from one simple item—the beaver hat. From the early seventeenth century to the middle of the nineteenth century, no proper European gentleman would appear in public without one. Hatters could scarcely keep up with demand. In 1760 alone, the Hudson Bay Company exported enough beaver pelts to England to make 576,000 hats.

In addition to beaver, the North American "skin game" provided pelts, called "brown gold," from marten, fox, and otter. They were turned into collars, sleeves, hems, gloves, and boots for men and women alike.

For two hundred years, the fur trade was *the* main trade of the North American wilderness. Animal pelts were the only things of value thought to exist there. As early as 1600, French pioneers paddled log canoes far into the American interior. They built trading

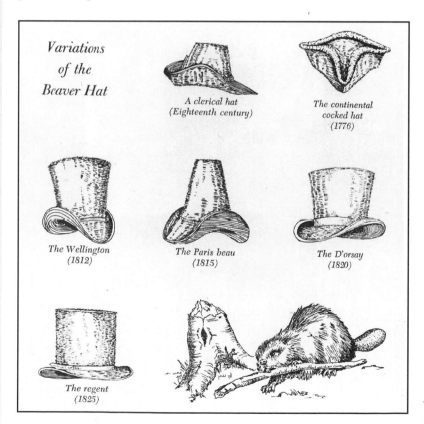

Variations of the Beaver Hat

A clerical hat
(Eighteenth century)

The continental
cocked hat
(1776)

The Wellington
(1812)

The Paris beau
(1815)

The D'orsay
(1820)

The regent
(1825)

Beaver hats and other garments were very popular in Europe. American trappers were eager to ravage the frontier to meet the increasing demand for beaver hides.

posts, collected pelts, and, in many cases, settled with Native American wives.

John Colter and the Early Trappers

The Missouri Fur Company was founded by a Spaniard named Manuel Lisa in 1807—less than a year after Lewis and Clark returned from the wilderness. Included in the company's roster of hunters were four veterans of the Lewis and Clark expedition: John Colter, George Drouillard, John Potts, and Peter Wiser. Colter was probably the most restless of the hunters. As the Corps of Discovery was floating homeward in 1806, Colter asked for a discharge from his duties so he could accompany two fur trappers heading back up the Missouri. Discharge in hand, Colter led the trappers back into the mountains he had so recently quit.

The three hunters wintered on the Yellowstone River. But some argument tore the trio apart. After a heated battle, one of the fur trappers, Joseph Dickenson, was abandoned by the other two. Dickenson, working alone during the spring thaw, harvested about a thousand pelts—ten a day. Without help, he skinned each animal, stretched each pelt, and packed them into bales, then loaded them on two dugout canoes lashed side by side. Still alone, he returned to St. Louis with $5,000 worth of pelts—a handsome sum in the days when a boatman made $120 a year. While this story has probably been exaggerated over the years, it is easy to see how such tales enticed farm boys, soldiers, and factory workers into the skin game.

Cashing In on Trappers

In the early nineteenth century, men who sold supplies to trappers published books to entice men to take up the trapper trade. One such merchant was Sewell Newhouse from Oneida, New York. His book, *The Trapper's Guide*, is described in historian Bil Gilbert's *The Trailblazers*.

"The Trapper's Guide: A manual of instructions for capturing all kinds of fur-bearing animals, and curing their skins; with observations on the fur trade, hints on life in the woods, and narratives of trapping and hunting excursions.

To aspiring 19th Century trappers, the title page above introduced the imaginative works of Sewell Newhouse who tried to cash in on the fur boom by his own unique methods. Newhouse's manual was dedicated to 'poor men who are looking out for pleasant work and ways of making money.' Not only was trapping profitable, but it would transform anyone into 'a stouter and healthier man.' Newhouse also advised that a man packing 50 pounds of equipment could make 'five hundred dollars in a trapping season.'

'Snowshoes are indispensable to the trapper wherever deep snows prevail,' Newhouse advised. He praised the dugout canoe as 'strong, serviceable, durable,' though many trappers found it heavy to carry. The birchbark canoe 'preferred on streams where portaging is necessary,' was sewn together and sealed with pine pitch.

Illustrations from *The Trapper's Guide* showed a highly romanticized view of a grubby, uncomfortable profession."

After he abandoned Dickenson, Colter himself was bobbing down the Missouri in June 1807 when he came across hunters of Lisa's Missouri Fur Company. Once again, instead of returning to civilization, Colter joined the company and headed back upstream. Toiling in heavy keel boats, Lisa's slow-moving party did not get to the Yellowstone and Big Horn Rivers until November. While the hunters were chopping cottonwood trees to build a stockade, Colter put on a thirty-pound pack and went to tell the Native Americans that more white hunters were in the area.

Colter then proceeded to take a lonesome, thousand-mile winter hike through some of the coldest and snowiest terrain in the world. He hiked out of present-day Cody, Wyoming, and up the valley of the Wind River. He met with some Crow Indians who took him west across the Continental Divide, into modern-day Jackson Hole. Colter then went over the Tetons and onto the Idaho slopes before returning back to Yellowstone Lake. There Colter reached a main trail used by the Bannock Indians, which he followed back to Lisa's fort in the spring of 1808. Colter's dazzling winter walk was considered to be one of the most extraordinary hikes ever taken in the Rockies.

The trappers of the Missouri Fur Company did not possess the self-confidence and wilderness skills of John Colter, however. While Colter was hiking through the snow Lisa obtained more financing and mobilized a new group of hunters. He was eager to push his exploitation of the mountains. Some feared attack by local Blackfeet Indians, but Lisa brushed aside objections. Colter led the men into Three Forks, in southwest Montana, in the spring of 1809, but some of the men suffered agonizing snow blindness. After erecting a crude fort, those who could scattered to trap. The Blackfeet hit twice, killing three men and stealing valuable equipment. One of those killed was George Drouillard, former member of the Corps of Discovery. A witness described his death: "His head was cut off, his entrails torn out, and his body hacked to pieces."[20] Colter had had enough. He finally went home.

After fighting off more Blackfeet attacks, the twenty men left in the company wintered near present-day St. Anthony, Idaho. Because of heavy snow and unceasing spring rains, game was scarce and trapping arduous. Crow Indians stole their horses. Hungry and disgusted, the group scattered. Some headed to Santa Fe. Others headed back to St. Louis.

The Fur Trappers' Rendezvous

Colter, Lisa, and the other fur trappers depended on the river town of St. Louis, Missouri, for their supplies. Located on the west bank of the Mississippi River, St. Louis became the reigning capital of the fur trade from 1815 to 1830. From its ports, steamboats transported people and supplies into beaver country. They carried back pelts by the ton. In those short fifteen years, over $3 million worth of animal pelts passed through the warehouses of that city.

St. Louis grew quickly, catering to the needs of thousands of weary trappers who had spent months in the wilderness. The waterfront was lined with taverns and gambling houses, which were filled with trappers, riverboat drivers, wagoners, drifters, and soldiers. Crime was rampant. Thieves, thugs, and kidnappers regularly prowled the town where there was no police force until 1838. On the hills above the town, wealthy fur merchants erected huge limestone homes furnished with mahogany, crystal, velvet, and lace.

One of the first men to successfully push the fur trade deep into the Rocky Mountains was William Ashley. A member of the St. Louis fur elite, Ashley ran an ad in 1822 looking for enterprising young men to go into the wilderness. He found sixty-two recruits to join his Rocky Mountain Fur Company. In 1823 Ashley became the first man to move a group of men and supplies into the Rockies by pack trains and wagons.

After opening up virgin wilderness in Green River country in Wyoming, Ashley told his men he would meet them in July 1825 with supplies from St. Louis. He would pay them and reoutfit them to trap for another year. Since no trapping was done in midsummer, the trappers could lounge around, gamble, and drink. Ashley also invited trappers who worked for other companies to come to the gathering, which came to be known as the "Rendezvous." Soon the Rendezvous was the best-known social and business gathering of the American mountain men.

The Rendezvous site changed from year to year. The mountain men met in Cache Valley, Utah, in 1826; Bear Lake, Utah, in 1827 and 1828; and Pierre's Hole, Idaho, in 1829. The Rendezvous provided the trapper with companionship, and a place to find new shoes, new clothes, female companionship, tobacco, and alcohol. After thirty days of drinking, fighting, loving, and gambling, the mountain men returned alone to the hardships of the wilderness.

A Mountain Man's Supplies

There was no single mold from which mountain men were made. But as a group they developed a style based on the demands of their work. While trappers' stories were often exag-

St. Louis was the western hub of the fur trade industry. The town grew rapidly as merchants set up shops and warehouses to deal with the trappers coming in from the frontier.

A typical mountain man was dressed in ragged furs and carried all the supplies of his trade on his person or on his horse, if he owned one.

gerations or tall tales, a convincing account of the typical mountain man comes from trader Rufus Sage, written in 1830.

His skin, from constant exposure, assumes the hue almost as dark as that of the Aborigine [Native American], and his features and physical structure attain a rough and hardy cast. His hair, through inattention, becomes long, coarse, and bushy, and loosely dangles upon his shoulders. His head is surmounted by a low crowned wool-hat, or a rude substitute of his own manufacture. His clothes are buckskin, gaily fringed at the seams with strings of the same material, and cut and made in a fashion peculiar to himself. The deer and buffalo furnish him the required covering for his feet. His waist is encircled with a belt of leather, holding encased his butcher-knife and pistols—while from his neck is suspended a bullet-pouch securely fastened to the belt in front, and beneath his right arm hangs a powder-horn, behind which, upon the strap attached to it are affixed his bullet-mould, ball-screw, wiper, awl, &c.[21]

In addition, the mountain man carried an extra set of leggings, several knives, a pipe, tobacco, and perhaps a book of poetry or the Bible. Spare locks and flints, twenty-five pounds of

Trappers and mountain men often spent months or years in the wilderness before returning to civilization. The demands of their work made them experts at living off the land.

gunpowder, a hundred pounds of lead (for bullets), and a rifle made up the rest of his baggage. The .60-caliber rifle was strong enough to knock down a buffalo, a grizzly bear, or a Blackfoot at two hundred yards.

Except for a little flour, some coffee, tea, and salt, the mountain man carried no food. Instead he lived off the land. Occasionally he might come across wild plums or nuts. In hard times he would eat whatever was available, including tree bark, roots, and his own boots. Meat was the trapper's main food. Any creature would do. Mountain men ate buffalo, deer, elk, bobcats, wolves, hawks, and even snakes.

Trapping Furs

Next to his guns, the mountain man's most important pieces of equipment were his traps. Each one cost about $12 to $16, and they were used during the two yearly trapping seasons. The first season was in fall, after the summer fur had become prime. The season lasted until ice and snow made work impossible. The second trapping season was in spring, after the ice broke up. The quality of fur deteriorated rapidly during warm weather. During both seasons, trappers worked all day in freezing water.

The standard procedure for a trapper was to wade in the muck of a swamp or pond. The trap was set underwater so that the animal would drown when caught. (Many beavers escaped by gnawing off their own trapped foot.) The trap was baited with a bit of greenery or scent. All that remained was for the trapper to check his traps every few days. Then he would haul a soaking-wet, forty-pound beaver carcass from the water and repeat the process.

When the trapper could no longer work in cold weather, he retired to a crude hut made from beaver skins. There he spent the winter preparing and finishing the skins so they could be used to make clothing.

Encountering Native Americans

Besides brutal weather and hunger, the trapper's greatest danger was being shot with an arrow or gun. Mountain man Jim Bridger once went about his business for three years with a long, barbed Blackfoot arrowhead buried in his back muscles. A missionary finally dug it out without any painkiller except, perhaps, a bottle of whiskey. Josiah Gregg, a Santa Fe trader, was accidentally shot in the arm by a member of his own trapping party. When gangrene set in, the arm had to be amputated with a hacksaw.

Wounds by gun or arrow were common in the lives of mountain men. This was largely due to the extreme hatred of many Native Americans, especially the Blackfeet and the Arikara. Some of the violence might have been avoided if the invading whites had been more diplomatic. Time and again, mountain men fought when they could have made peace. They lied where honesty would have served their interests, and they held their ground when they should have fled.

The friendlier natives of the plains, however, became an important part of the American fur trade. As skilled and courageous hunters, Native Americans exchanged pelts for blankets, guns, horses, whiskey, and other items.

Oftentimes trappers bought or kidnapped Native American girls to keep them company and take care of chores. Indian girls were regularly sold or traded by tribesmen. An especially detailed account of such a dismal transaction was written by artist George Catlin.

Their women are beautiful and modest . . . and if either Indian or white man wishes to marry the most beautiful girl in the tribe, she is valued only equal perhaps to

A Trapper's Dinner

The beaver provided money for the trappers. And it also provided food. David Coyner described the eating habits of Captain Williams in his 1850 book *The Lost Trapper.*

"Captain Williams subsisted principally upon the flesh of the beaver, which he caught in traps. This animal, when the hide is taken off, weighs about twelve pounds and its flesh, although a little musky, is very fine. Its tail, which is eight or ten inches long, is flat and oval, and is covered with scales about the size of those of a salmon fish. He separates it from the body of the beaver, thrusts a stick in one end of it, and places it before the fire with the scales on it. When the heat of the fire strikes through as to roast it, the tail is perfectly white, and very delicious. Next to the tail is the liver. This is another favorite dainty [treat] with the trapper."

two horses, a gun with powder and ball for a year, five or six pounds of beads, or a couple gallons of whiskey.[22]

The Fur Trapper's Payoff

Trappers faced endless hardships and dangers in exchange for money. A good trapper could come into town with three or four hundred pelts. A very good one might have twice that amount. After a mountain man unloaded his furs, he might have $2,000. This was at a time when a skilled worker such as a carpenter made about $1.50 a day.

Of course the money did not last long. Men who supplied trappers grew rich, while the trappers themselves remained poor. Trappers sold pelts at $2 to $4 a pound. Brokers resold them in St. Louis for $6 to $8 a pound.

The trapper was forced to sell his furs and buy his supplies at the Rendezvous, where prices were enormously inflated. Whiskey, an essential commodity, was bought in St. Louis at 30 cents a gallon, and resold at the Rendezvous for $24. The average price in St. Louis for tobacco, coffee, and sugar was 10 cents a pound. Lead and gunpowder were 7 cents a pound. At the Rendezvous, these items were sold for $2 a pound. If a trapper

Some native people were friendly and traded with the trappers. Other tribes were aggressive and attacked whites to steal their supplies, especially their firearms.

The Amazing Tales

John Colter was one of the most remarkable trappers to hike through the Rockies. Colter remained on friendly terms with many Native American tribes. But members of the Blackfeet hated the white trappers—a few Blackfeet had been killed by men of Lewis and Clark's Corps of Discovery. David Lavender describes Colter's run-ins with the Blackfeet in his book *The Rockies*.

"Colter's next lonesome foray led him into the Three Forks country. There he met a party of about 500 Flatheads [Indians] seeking buffalo. As he was starting to show them the wonders of [the fur] trade, a strong force of Blackfeet struck. The din of the conflict attracted several hundred Crows, who joined the battle with noisy relish.

What focused the hatred of the outnumbered Blackfeet, however, was the sight of a white man with their enemies. Wounded in the leg, Colter crawled into a bush and from its thin shelter pumped out balls as fast as he could load and prime his rifle. Finally the Blackfeet withdrew. Casualties on both sides left 'skulls and bones in vast numbers' littering the battlefield.

Later the Blackfeet caught Colter. They decided to amuse themselves by stripping him naked and ordering him to race for his life barefooted across the stony, cactus-spiked ground under a burning sun. He outdistanced all his pursuers but one, whom he killed. After hiding all night in the icy Madison River, he trudged without food or clothing 300 miles back to the fort."

had anything left after buying his supplies, he usually spent the rest on drinking, prostitutes, and gambling. The pay from eleven months of work would be gone after one month at the Rendezvous.

By the 1840s the mountain men were to be found in a vast area of the West. They traded their furs in St. Louis, Missouri, and they trapped beaver through the central Rockies of Wyoming, Colorado, Montana, and into the Great Basin of Utah. In less than thirty years, the mountain men ferreted out nearly every glade, lake, and stream in the terrain of the beaver.

Native Americans on the Frontier

In the mid-eighteenth century, the land between the Appalachians and the Mississippi River was populated by dozens of Native American tribes. The tribes fell into three major groupings: the Iroquois, the Algonquin, and the Southern Indian Confederation. The Native Americans roamed vast areas when they hunted. But they lived in permanent villages, usually near rivers where some of them farmed. Tribal boundaries overlapped, and tribes generally shared hunting grounds peacefully.

The woodland people were shrewd, intelligent, and sophisticated. But their culture was completely alien to that of Europeans. They were portrayed by whites as savages because of their beliefs in magic, personal glory, and the worth of other forest creatures.

For two hundred years, the Indian policies of American governments produced truces, treaties, bargains, and tragedy on both sides. Whites and Native Americans were locked in an uneasy state of dependence upon one another. White Americans were taught basic survival skills by the Native Americans. Later, the natives were deeply involved in the fur trade. And they were heavy consumers of European products such as blankets, knives, guns, and whiskey. Both sides agreed that there could be only one clear winner in the conquest of America. Early on, a governor of Virginia wrote: "Either we must cleere them or they us out oft the country."[23] Native Americans believed for many years that they were capable of doing the "cleering."

Native American Villages

The tribes of the forest lived in three distinct regions of the early Western frontier. The six nations of the Iroquois lived below Lakes Ontario and Erie in northern New York and Pennsylvania. The Algonquin occupied land from Tennessee and Virginia north to Canada. The five tribes of the Southern Indian Confederation spread across the Carolinas, Tennessee, northern Georgia, Alabama, Mississippi, and Florida. All three of these groups farmed the soil and lived in permanent villages. And they enjoyed cultures far more developed than those of the natives of the Great Plains and far West.

The Iroquois League was made up of Mohawk, Oneida, Onondaga, Cayuga, Seneca, and Tuscarora. They lived in villages with populations ranging from a few hundred to more than a thousand. The central feature of an Iroquois village was the longhouse—a building one hundred feet long and sealed with elm bark. The longhouse contained apartments for as many as twenty families and a public room with a cooking fire. The villages were protected by wooden stockades and surrounded by communal farms.

The Southern Nations were made up of Creek, Cherokee, Choctaw, and Chickasaw. They too lived in towns surrounded by stockades. The Southern Nations lived in wooden frame buildings covered in straw or thatch. Their small living quarters were often grouped around a larger central council house.

A Creek Indian house. Many of the southern tribes lived in log buildings similar to those of early white homesteaders.

The Algonquin tribes were Shawnee, Delaware, Miami, Potawatomies, and Ottawas. They lived in tepeelike dwellings made from animal hides, matting, or bark. Sometimes they built log cabins.

Native Agriculture

Because the natives had been growing crops in America for thousands of years, they were far better farmers than the pioneers. The Iroquois hybridized corn and grew more than a dozen varieties. They also grew five kinds of squash and ten types of beans. They added to their diet with dozens of types of roots, nuts, berries, and fruits from the forest.

The Southern Indians farmed tobacco, rice, melons, and sunflowers as well as beans, corn, and squash. The Cherokee quickly learned from whites how to breed cattle, horses, poultry, and swine. The Creek put aside rich tracts of land full of persimmons and chestnuts. These lands attracted bears, which would then be hunted after spiritual ceremonies.

The Algonquin grew pumpkins, peas, and watermelons along with their corn, beans, and squash. Those who lived near Lakes Erie and Huron caught a great abundance of fish. A French soldier wrote that the whitefish, sturgeon, trout, and pike came from "the purest water, the clearest and most pellucid [lucid] you could see anywhere."[24]

One of the Great Lakes tribes, the Chippewa, built wooden-frame lodges that were covered with hides or thatch.

Native American Beliefs

Almost all the woodland tribes believed in life after death for animals and human beings. They were deeply spiritual and held moral and religious beliefs far more rigorous than the average pioneer. Richard Dodge, a colonel in the U.S. army, wrote in 1877:

> No Christian, Moslem, or Bhudhist is more devoted to his religion, no High Churchman a greater stickler to form, than the Cheyenne Indian. His religion is mingled and interwoven with every phase of his life; and no project of any kind, governmental, social, or individual is ever undertaken without first obtaining the sense or disposition of the deities on the subject.[25]

Native Americans believed in a mysterious, supernatural force by which every human soul mingled with plants and animals. Because Indians felt a spiritual connection to

forest animals, they were outraged at white people's hunting practices. They had always lived in the endless forests and thought of ecological balance as natural and sacred.

The Pennsylvania tribes were particularly outraged by a backwoods lout named Black Jack Schwartz. In 1760 he headed a group of men who killed 109 wolves, 112 foxes, 41 panthers, 114 mountain cats, 17 black bears, 1 white bear, 198 deer, 111 buffalo, and more than 500 smaller animals. The whole mountain of flesh was piled up and set on fire. This purposeless slaughter was conducted simply as entertainment and was frowned upon even by white settlers. But the path of white settlement was commonly accompanied by a despoliation of forests, plants, and animals that drove many species to extinction.

Ownership of land was another foreign concept to Native Americans. They believed the earth was a sacred and living thing, and no person could own the rocks, trees, and animals. Tribes did fight each other for control of territories, but warfare typically occurred over hunting rights, not land ownership. Eventually, the natives were so outnumbered by settlers that they signed away great areas of wilderness to white people. In return they received guns, blankets, hatchets, and mirrors. But the treaties proved worthless in protecting the natives' lifestyle—every agreement was eventually violated by pioneers and the government.

The Fall of the Forest People

There was never an accurate count of Native Americans who lived east of the Mississippi in the eighteenth century. Some counts show an Iroquois population of ten thousand, the Southern Indians at thirty thousand, and a like number of Algonquin. Within those groups were perhaps two thousand to five thousand full-fledged warriors. No more than one thousand warriors ever fought together in a battle. Most Native American battle triumphs were accomplished by one hundred or fewer warriors.

The white man fought as he had in Europe. He fought to acquire land or to defend land he already had. He believed in meeting his enemy face-to-face and fighting until the death. These ideas seemed ridiculous to Native Americans. They believed in stealth when hunting and used those tactics in war. Native Americans fought for personal glory, not land ownership. They would die to prove they were brave, but they did not believe in dying for a cause.

Some Native Americans attacked white settlers whom they saw as encroaching on tribal lands.

By the late eighteenth century, the U.S. government simply considered the Native Americans a nuisance. The once-great Iroquois were the first to fall. Great throngs of Mohawk, Cayuga, and Seneca retreated to Canada. There were fewer than six thousand men, women, and children left behind. These weakened people surrendered great tracts of New York State in exchange for small cash settlements. By 1800 they were all pushed onto poverty-stricken reservations.

In Ohio, Indiana, and Illinois, the Algonquin were forced west into unknown territory. Those who did not die from disease, drink, or in battle were forced onto reservations in Mississippi. Thomas Jefferson expressed plans to introduce the natives to the "art of civilization, which would ultimately destroy the

The Trail of Tears

The fate of the Southern Indians was probably the harshest of all Native Americans, as they had followed the rules set up by white society. The Southern tribes embraced the "art of civilization" with great success. They adopted many of the laws, behaviors, and customs that were thrust upon them by white people. The Cherokee Nation lived peacefully in a farming society. By the mid-1820s, they owned a growing school system, 22,000 cattle, 10 cotton mills, 31 grist mills, and 700 looms. They also owned 1,300 black slaves. A Cherokee genius named Sequoia invented a tribal written language of 82 characters. He utilized it for the publication of a newspaper, the *Cherokee Phoenix*. In 1827 Cherokee delegates drew up a constitution modeled on that of the United States.

None of this protected the Cherokee from the thousands of pioneers streaming into eastern Georgia. The state of Georgia simply acquired the Cherokee lands by decree. The Supreme Court refused to reverse the decision. Finally the federal government ordered the removal of the Cherokee from their land. They, along with the Creek, Choctaw, and Chickasaw, were forced into the wilderness now known as Oklahoma.

They called the thousand-mile march the *Nuna-da-ut-sun'y*, or the Trail Where They Cried. A quarter of the men, women, and children on the forced march died along the way. Once they got to Oklahoma they were greeted with summer dust storms, winter snows, cholera, smallpox, and squalor.

Forced out of their homelands in the South, many of the Cherokee Nation died as they were relocated to reservations in Oklahoma.

The Plains Indians were excellent hunters, and they relied on herds of buffalo for food, clothing, tools, and shelter. Here, buffalo meat dries at an Arapaho camp.

distinctions between Savages and civilized people."[26] Congress authorized agencies to deal with the natives and expected Christian missionaries to alter Native American behavior. By 1809 over 100 million acres of land had been transferred by treaty from Native Americans to the federal government.

People of the Plains

After the Civil War ended in 1865, white settlers streamed into the lands west of the Mississippi. Thanks to the Homestead Act of 1862, any U.S. citizen could obtain free land for a small filing fee. Unfortunately, Native Americans were living on the land Congress had given away. On the eve of the white invasion, there were probably a quarter million Native Americans living on the Great Plains, in the Rockies, and in the intermountain region. In addition, there were about seventy-five thousand living along the Pacific coast. This represented about two-thirds of all Native Americans living in the United States.

The native people who lived on the Great Plains were wanderers who spent their time following great herds of buffalo. They were the Lakota, the Blackfeet, the Crow, the Cheyenne, and the Arapaho, among others.

There were millions of buffalo on the plains, and the natives used every part of the animal for their existence. Buffalo meat was their main food. The natives' dwellings, or tepees, were made by stretching buffalo skins over a straight pole frame. The tepees were decorated with geometrical designs, religious symbols, or pictures commemorating a warrior's deeds. They were blackened at the top where smoke from cooking fires escaped through a hole. Inside, the family slept on beds made of buffalo skins.

Spoons and cups were made from buffalo horn. Native women used bags made from buffalo skin to carry household items and food. They sewed clothes using buffalo thread. Water bottles were made from buffalo stomachs. Native children collected dried buffalo manure to feed campfires.

Thick, furry buffalo robes kept the natives warm in the frigid winter. But in the hot summer, children wore no clothing at all. Men wore just a breechcloth. Women wore deerskin dresses and leggings. Both men and

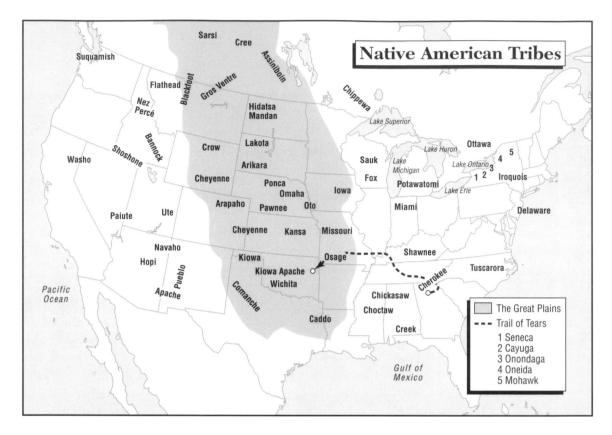

Native American Tribes

Map labels:
Sarsi, Cree, Assiniboin, Suquamish, Flathead, Blackfoot, Gros Ventre, Nez Percé, Hidatsa, Mandan, Chippewa, Lake Superior, Crow, Lakota, Ottawa, 5, Washo, Shoshone, Bannock, Arikara, Sauk, Lake Huron, Lake Ontario, 4, 3, 2, 1, Iroquois, Fox, Lake Michigan, Cheyenne, Ponca, Omaha, Iowa, Potawatomi, Lake Erie, Delaware, Paiute, Ute, Arapaho, Pawnee, Oto, Miami, Cheyenne, Kansa, Missouri, Navaho, Shawnee, Hopi, Kiowa, Osage, Tuscarora, Kiowa Apache, Wichita, Cherokee, Pueblo, Comanche, Apache, Chickasaw, Caddo, Choctaw, Creek, Pacific Ocean, Gulf of Mexico

Legend:
The Great Plains
- - - Trail of Tears
1 Seneca
2 Cayuga
3 Onondaga
4 Oneida
5 Mohawk

women decorated their clothes for special occasions. Men's shirts were covered with designs made with paint, beads, and porcupine quills. Women decorated their best dresses with beads, quills, and elks' teeth.

In the winter, buffalo grew thick coats. That winter fur was used to make mittens, caps, and moccasins. The skins of buffalo killed in the summer were used to make summer clothes. The delicate skin of buffalo calves was thin enough to make into underwear. Smoke-cured buffalo vests sometimes proved tough enough to deflect a bullet.

Before the coming of the Europeans in the seventeenth century, Native Americans traveled on foot. They did not have wheels, so they moved all their belongings on wooden frames dragged by dogs across the prairie. After several decades of trading with white men, the natives acquired horses. By the nineteenth century, the Plains Indians were expert horse riders.

The Plains people made their tools from wood and stone. Axes were stone heads affixed to wooden handles with strips of buffalo leather. Arrowheads were made from stone. When the white traders arrived on the scene, the natives traded furs for metal tools, steel axes and arrowheads, and guns.

A Meeting of the Plains People

In the hot summer, tribes of Plains people would gather along broad riverbanks. Women held considerable influence by virtue of doing most of the work around a camp. They were in charge of the important job of choosing lodging sites. The women looked for the best shade, nearness of water, firewood, grass on which to keep horses, and closeness to friends or prestigious members of the tribe.

The best spot was northeast of a giant cottonwood where the midday sun would be blocked off. The small green branches of the cottonwood were chopped off and served to make the fires smoky. This kept away the clouds of mosquitoes, gnats, and green flies that plagued the camp.

The women scoured the riverbanks for driftwood. They built brush arbors—cut poles set in the ground, bound across by light limbs, and covered with leafy branches on top. These arbors, open at the sides, provided cool shady places to cook, relax, and visit.

As several tribes gathered together, the men would dress in their finest clothing. Since making peace was the objective, war paint and shields were not in sight. Peacemaking was largely a matter of feasting, ceremony, and gift giving, all designed to demonstrate goodwill.

The tribes did not come together often because the numerous horses would quickly eat all the grass in the area. These gatherings were rare opportunities to meet old friends, exchange news, feast, joke, play, gamble, and trade horses.

Naked children ran squealing between the tepees, riding stick horses. Boys a little older set out on hunting and fishing expeditions, carrying half-sized spears and bows and arrows. The older boys put on riding demonstrations, hanging on the side of a galloping horse, and swinging down to pick up an object from the ground. The girls helped their mothers or played with dolls. Older girls showed off their beadwork and demonstrated their braiding skills.

Games and sport filled the days. Women played an awl game—sort of a board game

Buffalo hunting fed the Plains Indians, and it also improved the riding and fighting skills of the young hunters.

Sports were common to most Native American tribes. Here, Choctaws play a ball game.

using blankets, special sticks, and awls used for perforating hides. Men set up courses for horse races and gambled recklessly on the results.

All this activity was accompanied by chants and songs. Drummers brought out painted drums, and social dances sprang up around them. Women danced in circles or in a snakelike parade. Men sang in deep voices, women in higher registers. Hand rattles made from gourds or hides swished out the measure to the drums.

The Government and the Plains People

Such activity might have taken place around 1840, on the Arkansas River, not far from the white pioneers' wagon tracks known as the Santa Fe Trail. In 1840 the natives saw no threat from the trade that moved across that trail. In fact, that year, a French trader had bought sixty-seven thousand buffalo robes, all of them tanned and skinned by Native Americans. In return the natives received blankets, bolts of bright cloth, cheap guns, three hundred butcher knives, and nine thousand pounds of beads. At this time, the Plains culture was at its peak of development. The horse-mounted natives were raiding and trading over vast areas.

But within the next twenty years, the population of the United States would swell to 30 million. The U.S. government, however, maintained: "The Indians residing within the United States are so far independent that they live under their own customs and not under the laws of the United States, that their rights upon the lands which they inhabit or hunt are secured to them by the boundaries defined in amicable treaties between the United States and themselves."[27]

The security did not last long. Native Americans found that lands granted to them "forever" were quickly given to white settlers. As soon as one treaty was signed, the government would ask for more land and another treaty. The government usually offered to pay for the land in yearly installments of food, guns, blankets, and axes.

Sometimes the government changed how much it would pay the natives. When the tribes came to collect their agreed-upon payment, they often found it was not as large as expected. Or it was of such poor quality as to be useless. This could spell disaster when winter was approaching and a tribe suddenly found itself without enough supplies. Many attacks on white settlers were by natives who had not gotten the food and blankets promised to them in treaties. The U.S. government responded by sending in the army.

Making Buffalo Robes

Making a buffalo robe took weeks of skillful labor. After a buffalo was killed, women of the tribe carefully stripped off its skin. Then they stretched it out on the ground, flesh-side up, and fastened it down with wooden pegs. With sharp bone or stone scrapers, the women scraped off any flesh that was left on the skin. The skin could not be left out in the sun to dry or it would become hard and brittle. The skin was kept wet with water in which buffalo brains had been soaked. It was rubbed every day for ten days so that it would become very soft. When they were finished, the fur was silky, warm, and supple.

The Plains people valued white buffalo robes the most. These were very difficult to find. A hunter might come across an albino buffalo perhaps once in a lifetime. White buffalo robes were thought to resemble soft, puffy clouds. Another valuable buffalo robe was called a "beaver" robe. To make a robe of this type, women pulled out the long, coarse buffalo hairs, leaving only the short ones. This gave the skin the appearance of beaver fur.

The End of the Buffalo

There may have been as many as 30 to 50 million buffalo roaming the plains when the white settlers first arrived. By the 1870s, Native Americans and the U.S. army had been fighting a series of skirmishes for ten years. When a large number of white buffalo hunters showed up on the Texas Panhandle in 1874, they represented an immediate threat to the natives' food supply.

For many years, white people were not interested in the buffalo. Their hides were not as strong as cowhide, so buffalo leather was not desirable. Two advances in technology, however, doomed the buffalo. A new method of tanning hides made buffalo as useful as leather. Buffalo robes became very fashionable in Europe. At the same time, high-powered Sharps rifles with telescopic sights went into production. These guns could kill a full-grown buffalo at six hundred yards.

The buffalo plains became a vast slaughterhouse. A top marksman could bag two hundred animals a day—enough to keep fifteen buffalo skinners busy. At the height of the hunt, forty thousand hides a day were shipped from Dodge City, Kansas, alone. By 1886 a herd of 50 million buffalo had been reduced to fewer than one thousand animals.

Army officers encouraged hunters to kill buffalo on native lands. They correctly figured that the slaughter of the buffalo would starve the natives and force them onto reservation land. General Philip Sheridan praised the buffalo hunters for "destroying the Indian's commissary. For the sake of lasting peace, let them kill, skin, and sell until they have exterminated the buffalo. Then your prairies will be covered with speckled cattle and the festive cowboy."[28]

Wagons loaded with buffalo hunters arrived on the prairies. They were followed by

Chief Seattle's Speech

Chief Seattle was the leader of the Suquamish people, a fishing tribe in Washington State. As he saw his way of life falling to the white people in 1854, he gave this eloquent speech. (The edited version here is from the Internet site maintained by the Suquamish tribe.)

"Yonder sky that has wept tears of compassion on our fathers for centuries untold. . . . My words are like the stars that never set. What Seattle says, the great chief, Washington, can rely upon. . . .

The great, and I presume also good, white chief sends us word that he wants to buy our lands but is willing to allow us reserve enough to live on comfortably. This indeed appears generous, for the red man no longer has rights that he need respect. . . .

There was a time when our people covered the whole land as the waves of a wind-ruffled sea cover its shell-paved floor. But that time has long since passed away with the greatness of tribes now almost forgotten. . . .

Your God loves your people and hates mine; . . . he has forsaken his red children; he makes your people wax strong every day, and fill the land; while our people are ebbing away like a fast-receding tide, that will never flow again. The white man's God cannot love his red children or he would protect them. . . .

Our religion is the traditions of our ancestors, the dream of our old men, given by the great Spirit, . . . and is written in the hearts of our people. . . .

It matters but little where we pass the remainder of our days. They are not many.

The Indian's night promises to be dark. No bright star hovers about the horizon. . . . A few more moons, a few more winters, and not one of all the mighty hosts that once tilled this broad land or that now roam in fragmentary bands . . . will remain to weep over the tombs of a people once as powerful and as hopeful as your own. . . .

Every part of this country is sacred to my people. Every hillside, every valley, every plain and grove has been hallowed by some fond memory or some sad experience of my tribe. . . .

The very dust under your feet responds more lovingly to our footsteps than to yours, because it is the ashes of our ancestors, and our bare feet are conscious of the sympathetic touch, for the soil is rich with the life of our kindred. . . .

At night when the streets of your cities and villages shall be silent, and you think them deserted, they will throng with the returning hosts that once filled and still love this beautiful land."

Buffalo once covered the plains. However, as buffalo robes became fashionable in Europe and the military saw the weakening of the herds as a way to starve the Indians off their homelands, these animals were slaughtered in great numbers.

wagon loads of skinners. Behind them they left piles of buffalo meat and bones to rot in the hot prairie sun. Poor settlers moved in to take the bones, which were used for fertilizer and fine china dishes.

The natives looked on in horror. They tried to drive the buffalo hunters away but failed. In 1883 a museum expedition came to the West to prepare a display of stuffed buffalo. They could only find two hundred of the animals. The buffalo that were once the living carpet of the prairies were gone. And the glory days of the Plains people were not far behind.

4 Miners and Forty-Niners

For eons, little streams drained down from the High Sierra in California. At first the streams were only known to Native Americans. Later, Spaniards and Mexicans discovered them. Then came the hardy hunters and trappers looking for beaver, muskrat, and otter. The mountain men loved the sweet, clean waters, especially after crossing California's parched desert.

Then in the late 1840s the calm was shattered by one of the greatest mass adventures of all times. The event was triggered by a one-paragraph item in a San Francisco newspaper called the *Californian*. Printed on March 15, 1848, the article read:

GOLD MINE FOUND—In the newly made raceway of the saw-mill recently erected by Captain Sutter, on the American fork, gold had been found in considerable quantities. One person brought thirty dollars worth to New Helvetica, gathered in a short time. California, no doubt, is rich.[29]

News of the discovery spread like wildfire. People from all over the world began pouring into northern California. They came from the East Coast by boat. This journey was a thirteen-thousand-mile, twelve-month trip on a boat that sailed down the east coast of South and Central America, around Cape Horn, and up the western edge of the Americas to San Francisco. Others sailed south along the east coast of Central America, walked across the steaming swamps of Panama, and sailed north up the west coast to California.

Most people without means walked and rode horses overland along the Oregon and Overland Trails. Five thousand emigrants walked to Sacramento on the Overland Trail in 1848. After the discovery of gold in 1849, thirty thousand made that journey. In 1850 fifty thousand emigrants crossed to California on the Overland Trail.

Those who came were mostly men lured by the passion to get rich quick. They left behind their homes, their families, and their businesses, and staked all they had on getting to California. Many did not survive the hardships of the long journey. Others who did survive and made their way to mining towns and camps ended up broke. Few found wealth or happiness.

Abandoning San Francisco

Gold fever first swept through the sleepy town of San Francisco, which at the time had a population of about ten thousand. People believed anyone could become rich by simply picking up gold nuggets or digging them out of rocks with a pocketknife. People left for the diggings on foot, horse, mule, wagon, or any type of boat that would float up the Sacramento River. Workers quit their jobs, houses were left vacant, stores were simply abandoned. Merchants hung up signs that read: "Gone to the diggings. Help yourself. Put your money in the cash drawer and take your own change."[30]

The mayor of Monterey, Walter Colton, tells how gold fever spread:

Another bag of gold from the mines and another spasm in the community. It was brought down from a sailor on the Yuba River, and contains a hundred thirty-six ounces. My carpenters, at work on the schoolhouse, on seeing it, threw down their saws and planes, shouldered their picks, and are off to the Yuba.

A vast sea of humanity swarmed onto the gold-fields. Colton describes the scene:

Some fifty thousand persons are drifting up and down these slopes of the great Sierra, of every hue, language, and clime,

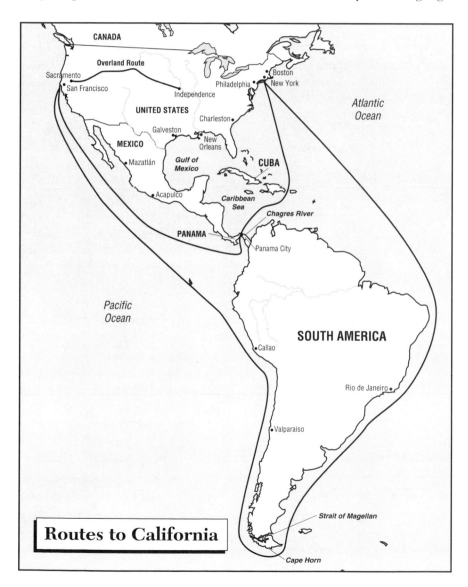

Routes to California

A view of San Francisco a year before the strike at Sutter's Mill. This town would lose much of its population to gold fever, though it would recover quickly as people from all over the nation flocked here to outfit themselves for prospecting.

tumultuous and confused as a flock of wild geese. Some are with tents, some without; some have provisions, some are on their last ration; some carrying crowbars and pickaxes and spades, some washbowls and cradles; some hammers and drills, and enough powder to blow up the rock of Gibralter.[31]

Prices around the goldfields soared. Flour sold for $800 a barrel, sugar $400. Eggs were $3 apiece, and a pound of bread cost $2. Shovels were sold for $100. This was at a time when a skilled worker made about $2 a day.

The Work of Mining

When newcomers got to the mines, they were taught by the old-timers how to pan for gold. They began by digging up a quantity of what they hoped was gold-bearing sand. Dumping this mixture into Indian baskets, tin cups, old

hats, or blankets, the miner added a steady stream of water to wash out the dirt. Gold, being heavier, sank to the bottom. Panning required patience, skill, and much physical strain. Miners had to stoop or squat near the water's edge, constantly shaking or rotating the heavy pan.

Though not as thorough as panning, rocking a cradle was faster, and quickly became popular with the miners. A "rocker," or "cradle," was a wooden box mounted on rockers, similar to a baby's cradle. It was open at the lower end with a coarse grate or sieve at its head. Cleats were nailed across the bottom to catch the gold. Three or more people worked the rocker, digging dirt and supplying buckets. This, too, was hard work.

No matter the method, few miners simply stumbled onto riches. It was highly exacting work. A miner known as T. T. Johnson wrote:

At the edge of the stream, or knee deep and waist deep in water as cold as melted ice and snow, some were washing gold while the rays of the sun were pouring down on their heads with an intensity exceeding anything we ever experienced at home. The thirst for gold and the labor of acquisition over-ruled all else; complete silence reigned among the miners. All the sympathies of our common humanity, all the finer and nobler attributes of our nature seemed lost, buried beneath the soil they were eagerly delving, or swept away with the rushing waters that revealed the shining treasure.[32]

Prospectors pan for gold. The search for gold was backbreaking labor often with very little reward.

Miners and Mining Towns

Although there were many languages spoken in the mining towns, two-thirds of the people were American. Most of them were young men who were rarely called by their real names. They were known as Yankee Jimmy, Sailor Jack, Fuzzy, Hatchet, or Hell-Roaring Jo. One man who continually got lost was called Compass. A man who was a fancy dresser was named Frippery Jim.

It was not healthy or polite to inquire too closely into a man's past. A popular ditty in the goldfields sums up the miners' attitudes about their past lives.

Oh, what was your name in the states?

Was it Thompson, or Johnson, or Bates?

Did you flee for your life or murder your wife?

Say, what was your name in the states?[33]

Miners dressed in various styles. Some wore clothes popular in the East, such as top hats, overcoats, and suits. Others wore the clothing of cowboys—deerskin breeches, sombreros, and bandannas. Many forty-niners wore flannel shirts of red and blue. Woolen pantaloons were usually tucked into the tops of high boots. Almost everybody wore boots because they were constantly wading in and out of water. A low-crowned, wide-brimmed hat completed the outfit.

Mining towns were mainly tents and rough log or bark structures. They were often built into a hollow at the side of a creek, and surrounded by high, steep hills. Towns were thrown up anywhere gold was found and torn down as quickly when the gold was exhausted.

The names of mining towns were no less colorful than the names of the miners themselves. At one time California boasted such towns as Poker Flat, Chucklehead Diggings, Git Up and Git, Humbug Canyon, Poverty Hill, You Bet, Squabbletown, and Mad Ox Ravine.

Boardinghouses, restaurants, saloons, casinos, and houses of prostitution settled in next to one another. Storekeepers set up flimsy shacks to supply the miners. Goods were expensive because they had to be hauled in from San Francisco.

The forty-niners lived on simple fare. Flour, salt, and pork were their staples. Other essentials included beans, rice, dried apples, coffee, sugar, molasses, and baking soda to make bread. Occasionally fresh meat was supplied by drovers who brought in herds of cattle or hogs from San Francisco. Hunters sold game such as bear, deer, elk, or rabbit. Fresh meat spoiled quickly so salted meat was preferred. Tobacco and alcohol were also necessities for most miners.

Money seemed to have no value to the miners. They spent their gold dust recklessly. Miners worked hard and played hard. Sundays were filled with wrestling matches, jumping matches, and other athletic contests. There were bull fights, cockfights, and bear fights. All, of course, were accompanied by gambling. Miners also gathered to drink, play cards, and tell tall tales. As time went by, stagecoaches brought in professional entertainers and actors. The entertainment-starved miners were treated to Shakespeare, vaudeville acts, minstrel shows, and circuses.

Any person who could play a guitar, banjo, harmonica, or accordion was treated to free drinks. Frequently dances were held, even though there were no women for miles around. Men with long beards in heavy boots and flannel shirts danced together, their revolvers and bowie knives clanking in their belts.

That Long Walk West

Before men could realize their dreams panning for gold, they had to get to California. Many did not survive the very beginning of the trip in Independence, Missouri, where the forty-niners gathered to go west. In his 1923 book, *The Argonauts of '49*, Octavius Thorndike Howe describes the pitfalls waiting for the unwary in Independence.

"The time required to make the journey under favorable conditions was one hundred days and the distance covered two thousand miles. The journey was made in parties numbering ten to twenty wagons. The start from Independence could not be made until the first of May. On April 17, 1849, there were three thousand men camping near the town waiting for the grass to grow. The encampment had the appearance of a great fair. Peddlers shouted their wares, dance halls and drinking saloons abounded, while the crowd of gamblers relieved the unwary of their cash. This wait in Independence was one of the bad features of the South Pass route, for not only did men often lose the money they had provisioned for the trip, but they drank so hard and lived in such an unsanitary way that dysentery and cholera were always prevalent and took heavy toll before departure."

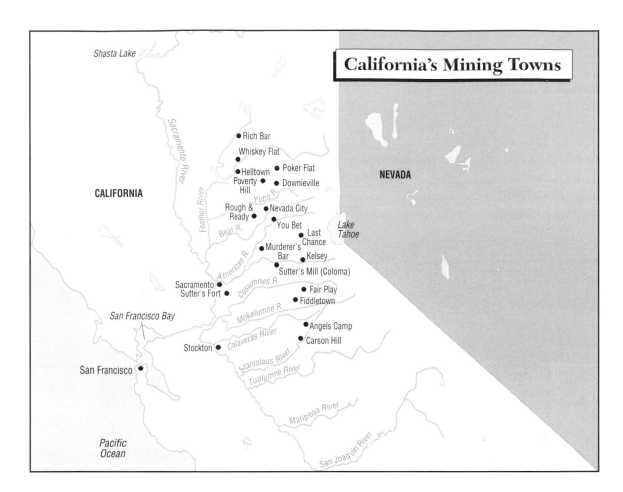

The Miner's Hardships

The mining season was limited by heat, cold, snow, and rain. The best months were April, May, June, October, and November. In the summer, miners worked "short" eight-hour days, resting from 11 A.M. to 4 P.M. Rain usually began in November and fell constantly until March. Holes collapsed, camps flooded, and miners were left without any source of income. Those who stayed in the mines year-round usually had no choice.

Miners were far from healthy. They slept on the ground and worked up to eighteen hours a day. A miner named Daniel Woods wrote of his life:

We made $3 each day. This life of severe hardship and exposure had affected my health. Our diet consisted of hard bread, flour, which we eat half cooked and salt with pork, with occasionally a salmon which we purchase off the Indians. Vegetables are not to be procured. Our drinking water comes down to us thoroughly impregnated with the mineral substances washed through the thousand cradles above us.

We must work. In sunshine and rain, in warm and cold, in sickness and health, successful or not successful, early and late, it is work, work, WORK! Work or perish! The miners work with the rain

The little money miners did make was typically lost to drinking or gambling when they returned to town.

falling fast upon them. They work not for gold but for bread. Lawyers, doctors, clergymen, farmers, soldiers, deserters, good and bad, from England, from America, from China, from the Islands—all, all, work at their cradles.[34]

Miners suffered from back trouble, sore hands and feet, dysentery, rheumatism, malaria, diarrhea, chills, and fevers. Scurvy was common because vegetables were rare. Miners seldom had time to bathe, shave, or cut their hair. They fought a running battle with fleas, vermin, and lice.

When a miner died, he was wrapped in a blanket and thrown into a deep hole. Burial services were short so the living could get back to work. In one instance, the funeral of a more respected miner, the services went on too long. The mourners began absentmindedly fingering the loose dirt thrown up from the grave— ever searching for gold. When a chunk was discovered, the dead miner was lifted out of his

grave and buried elsewhere. The funeral party immediately began prospecting the diggings.

Women's Lives During the Gold Rush

Women were few in the rough mining camps. Some men went years without a woman's companionship. When one forty-niner, G. W. Thissell, heard that a white woman had arrived at Snow's Camp, he wrote:

I put on my best jeanpants, a pair of alligator boots, and a red flannel shirt. I struck out on foot to see the wonderful creature. When I arrived at Snow's Camp, it was late in the day and Mrs. Snow kept a restaurant. I ordered dinner at $1.50. It was dark long before I reached home, and should I live to be a hundred—I shall never forget the day I walked 16 miles to see a woman in California.[35]

Forty-niners on their way home passed through San Francisco. The town had grown from ten thousand in 1848 to forty-five thousand by the end of 1849. Gambling houses and saloons opened by the score. By 1853 there were forty-five houses of prostitution in the city.

Women came flocking to San Francisco in large numbers. They worked as bartenders and card dealers to lure men into the saloons. Some women came as actresses and performers. The unskilled or unwary often ended up as prostitutes.

"Respectable" women had to work hard to survive. They were employed running boardinghouses, cooking, and laundering. The demand for their services was so great they could make a good living by their hard labor.

Mary Jane Megquier wrote a letter to her daughter in Maine in 1850. In it she described her day's work feeding the boarders at the San Francisco hotel she owned with her husband:

At seven o'clock I get up and make the coffee, then I make the biscuits, then I fry the potatoes, then broil three pounds of steak, and as much liver. At eight the bell rings and they are eating until nine. I do not sit until they are nearly all done. After breakfast I bake six loaves of bread, then four pies, or a pudding. . . . [For lunch] we have lamb, beef, and pork, baked turnips, beets, potatoes, radishes, salad, and that ever-lasting soup. Every day, at two, for tea we have hash, cold meat,

Makeshift towns sprang up around prospecting sites. When claims failed to yield gold, however, the towns would be left vacant as the miners moved on.

bread and butter sauce and some kind of cake and I have cooked every mouthful that has been eaten excepting one day and a half that we were on a steamboat excursion. I make six beds every day and do the washing and ironing you must think I am very busy and when I dance all night I am obliged to trot all day and had I not the constitution of six horses I should have been dead long ago.[36]

The account was not unusual for women in mining towns. Narcissa Whitman wrote of having to keep house for ten or more "loose" men. "At times it seems I cannot endure any longer . . . the cooking and eating room is al-ways filled with five or more men. They are so filthy they require a great deal of cleaning wherever they go, and this wears out a woman very fast."[37]

The End of the Forty-Niners

In 1853 over 100,000 forty-niners swarmed across California. Nearly every stream and river from Shasta in the north to Mariposa in the south had felt the dish of the prospector's pan. That year $67 million was taken from those mountains. Yet by that time, though no one wanted to admit it, the big bonanza was ending. The easy-to-reach placers were ex-

In the mining regions, the population of men greatly outnumbered that of women. The arrival of a woman to a mining camp was a special occasion.

Miners and Native Americans

California Native Americans suffered greatly because of the gold rush. The forty-niners had little respect for or understanding of them. Worse yet, their lands lay on the rich diggings. Caught with gold fever, miners were in no mood to tolerate opposition in their drive to riches. They did not care whose streams they were fouling or whose sacred burying ground they were digging up. In 1855 army lieutenant Philip Sheridan wrote about the Pit River tribe, excerpted here from Laurence I. Seidman's book *The Fools of '49*.

"Indians are always hungry, but these poor creatures were particularly so, as their usual supply of food had grown very scarce. In former years salmon were very abundant in the streams of the Sacramento Valley, and every fall they took great quantities of these fish and dried them for winter use. But alluvial mining has of late years defiled the water of the different streams and driven the fish out."

Between 1849 and 1852, open warfare broke out in many places. When the California legislature appropriated $500,000 to "settle" the Indian problem, miners joined state militias. They found they could get good pay to hunt down Native Americans and kill them. By the end of the 1800s, northern California's Native Americans had met the same fate as Eastern tribes.

hausted. Tailings left by previous miners had been worked over two, three, even four times.

For the next quarter century, over $978 million worth of gold would be mined in California. The gold was still in the hills, but the average miner with his pack mule could not find it. Sophisticated engineering skills and heavy machinery came in to take the place of the pan and cradle.

Most miners cashed in their chips and began to mine California's other riches. During those half-dozen years of the gold rush, over 250,000 people moved to California where 14,000 had lived before. In a few short years, California had become settled and civilized. San Francisco had grown overnight from a quiet town full of whaling boats and schooners to a major center of finance and commerce. Men who struck it rich during the gold rush took center stage in world politics, agriculture, and manufacturing.

Mining the Mountains

No sooner had the gold rush come to a halt for the forty-niners than it began all over again for the "fifty-niners." In January 1859, a miner named George Jackson found gold in the south fork of Clear Creek, thirty miles west of Denver, Colorado. Jackson pulled $1,900 worth of gold from the mine and sold his stake in it for a modest sum. (The Clear Creek area would yield over $100 million worth of gold for the next sixty years.)

Soon, the Rockies were inundated with 100,000 prospectors. They had come willy-nilly in response to exaggerated reports in Eastern newspapers. As in the previous gold rush, few were prepared for the hazards they faced. They painted their wagons with the slogan "Pike's Peak or Bust."

Jackson's strike opened a new chapter in the settlement of the Western frontier. For the next fifty years, the nation's interior from the Rockies to the Sierra Nevada and the Cascades, and from Canada to Mexico, would be crisscrossed by legions of miners. They would toss up outposts on unpopulated lands that had been ignored during the rush to California.

No one knows how many miners took part in the great adventure. But by 1866 there were more than six hundred far-flung mining districts across the West. The incredible Comstock Lode in the Washoe Mountains of Nevada, discovered in June 1859, yielded nearly $400 million in gold and silver by the end of the century. But before the extent of the riches was known, Henry Comstock sold his portion of the lode for $11,000 and two jackasses, beasts that Comstock later claimed cost him $1.5 million each. Comstock committed suicide a few years later.

In the Black Hills of South Dakota two prospectors named Moses and Fred Manuel founded the Homestead Mine in 1876. This mine, one of the richest in the world, gave up over $1 billion worth of precious metals. The Native Americans who lived there and considered this land holy were slaughtered by land-hungry prospectors.

The densest concentration of gold was in Cripple Creek, Colorado. In an area of six square miles, 475 mines produced $360 million worth of gold in 25 years. Thanks to the Clear Creek and Cripple Creek mines, Colorado became the greatest gold-producing state, surpassing California in 1870. Colorado gained statehood six years later.

Mines and mining structures transformed the landscape around Cripple Creek, Colorado. The great mineral strikes in this region helped Colorado gain statehood.

A Miner's Gritty Language

Miners had a language all their own when it came to describing the details of their gritty work. Robert Wallace compiled a list of miners' terms in his book *The Miners*.

"Amalgamation: a process of using mercury to collect fine particles of gold or silver.

Bonanza: an exceptionally rich vein of gold.

Claim: a parcel of land in a gold field that a person was legally entitled to mine because he had staked it out and recorded the title.

Claim jumping: stealing someone else's claim.

Fool's gold: pyrite, a lustrous heavy, yellow mineral, which unlike real gold is hard and brittle.

Grubstaking: supplying a prospector with food and gear in return for a share of the findings.

Gumbo: the bane of a miner's existence—wet, sticky, clay.

Lode: a clearly defined vein of rich ore. The principal vein was called a 'mother lode.'

Placer: a deposit of sand, dirt, or clay, often in an active or ancient stream bed, containing fine particles of gold or silver, which could be mined by washing. Rhymes with 'passer.'

Salting: planting rich ore samples in an unprofitable mine to attract unwary buyers.

Sourdough: an experienced prospector, traditionally one who had the foresight to save a wad of fermenting dough to leaven the following day's bread.

Widow-maker: a compressed-air drill, used to bore holes for dynamite in hard rock. Prolonged inhalation of the fine dust created by early models of the drill subjected miners to a deadly lung disease called silicosis."

But as new mining methods took hold, former independent miners soon found themselves working for large companies. Forced to live in towns owned by the companies, these miners worked in mine shafts sunk hundreds of feet into the earth. The new machinery made miners' lives even more miserable than before. Temperatures in the mines were over one hundred degrees. Cave-ins were frequent. Pay was $3 a day. And deep-rock mining—which required extensive blasting, digging, and chemical processing—was an even greater destroyer of the land's natural ecology.

By the end of the century, America's mining industry was dominated by giant corporations. The only reminder of the miners of '49 and '59 were the thousands of abandoned ghost towns and crumbling graveyards that dotted the West.

Ribbons of Steel

In the three decades before the Civil War, Americans had built a vast railroad system across the eastern United States. By the 1860s, the iron fingers of the rail system reached into the edge of the frontier, from Wisconsin to Texas. With the riches of gold and silver to be found in the far West, Americans were anxious to expand the rails westward.

The railroad train was also the perfect instrument for those who believed in Manifest Destiny. As Senator Thomas Hart Benton put it when proposing a cross-country rail system:

Emigrants would flock upon [the railroad] like pigeons to their roosts, tear open the bosom of the virgin soil, and spring into existence the long line of farms and houses, of towns and villages, of orchards, fields, and gardens, of churches and schoolhouses, of noisy shops, clattering mills, and thundering forges, and all that civilization affords to enliven the wild domain from Mississippi to the Pacific.[38]

The first railroad west of the Mississippi River was a five-mile road that ran west of St. Louis in 1852. That five-mile stretch of tracks would grow to seventy-two thousand miles by 1890. To make it happen, Congress would grant more than 116 million acres of the West to railroad companies while advancing $64 million in bonds to build roads. No longer would it take pioneers three months to walk across the continent. A train rumbling out of New York would reach San Francisco a mere eighty-four hours later.

The Dream of a Cross-Country Railroad

Early believers in a transcontinental railroad were considered dreamers. Building a sixteen-hundred-mile-long railroad that could run from Missouri to the Pacific was thought impossible. Within that expanse rose two mountain chains scraping the skies with fourteen-thousand-foot peaks. In winter, the passes were covered in snowdrifts up to forty feet deep. Between the mountains lay a desert of hundreds of miles where there was no water and wood to fire the locomotives. It seemed beyond human ability to impose a series of cuts, fills, tunnels, bridges, freight yards, roundhouses, and passenger depots on such a wilderness.

In the 1840s, in spite of the naysayers, momentum began building in Congress for such an engineering miracle. Of course most congressmen had never been west of the Mississippi so had no idea what they were proposing. Those from southern states wanted the route to run through the South. Those from the plains wanted a route out of St. Louis. Congressmen from Chicago wanted a northern route.

Meanwhile lobbyists were pressing Congress for grants of land for these roads. Land was something the government owned in almost measureless quantities. In 1850 Presi-

America's First Railroad

On January 15, 1831, America's first passenger locomotive wheezed out of Charleston, South Carolina. For six months, the machine named *Best Friend of Charleston* rattled and rolled twenty miles between the city and a few nearby towns. One day, the train's fireman, annoyed by the hiss of escaping steam, fastened down the engine's safety valve. This ended the vital protection provided by the valve. The *Friend* and the fireman blew up together.

America's other early engines had similar sad records. They spewed sparks, jerked people off their seats, and jumped their tracks when they hit a sharp curve. Because of the noise they made, people called them "puffers." But locomotive designs improved rapidly. By 1837 Henry Campbell built the first eight-wheel locomotive. By 1856 refinements included a cowcatcher, a headlight, and a spark-killing smokestack. By the time the transcontinental railroad was built across the West, steam locomotives were the most refined machines of their day.

dent Millard Fillmore gave 2.6 million acres to the Illinois Central and similar acreage to a railroad in Alabama. This quickly snowballed into one of the greatest land giveaways in history. Between 1850 and 1860, about 20 million acres of federal land were granted to private railroad companies, most of them east of the Mississippi.

Building the Union Pacific

In 1860 Abraham Lincoln was elected president. One of his campaign pledges was to build a railroad to the Pacific. In 1862, while the Civil War was raging, Lincoln signed into law the Pacific Railway Act. It authorized two companies to build a transcontinental railroad. The Union Pacific was to build westward from the Missouri River. This company was set up under federal charter, and stock was sold to raise $100 million. The Central Pacific, a private company, was to build eastward from Sacramento.

The Railway Act awarded the Central Pacific Company ten miles of land on either side of the track for each mile laid. Congress also gave the companies $16,000 a mile for track on the plains, and $48,000 per mile through the Sierra Nevada and Rockies.

On December 2, 1863, ground was finally broken on the bleak Nebraska prairie. But the Civil War slowed plans to build the line. Labor was hard to find, and the eastern line stalled in the middle of Iowa for months. While waiting, the builders of the road persuaded Congress to double the land grant. When the war ended in 1865, work began in earnest.

Working on the Railroad

The politics and planning of the railroad were completed. Now the dangerous, backbreaking, and brawling work of building the lines was to begin.

The Union Pacific work crews were assembled from Civil War veterans, freed slaves, Irish and German immigrants, Mormons, Shoshones, Paiutes, Washos, and Chinese. When labor was short, crews took on a few Native American women. All were paid about $35 a month.

Working in several shifts, the workers laid two to five miles of track a day. They filled in ravines, built trestles across rivers and valleys, and punched holes through mountains. And they did it all using their own muscle power.

There were four hundred rails per mile of road. Each five-hundred-pound rail was put in place by five men who called themselves "rust eaters." Another five men drove thirty spikes into each rail, with three blows per spike. All the while the men fought off rain, sleet, snow, bitter cold, and Lakota and Cheyenne.

Workers often sang while they swung shovels and spike hammers. The builders promised the men extra tobacco if they could build a mile of track a day. Later, workers were promised an extra half-day's pay to build a mile and a half per shift. In 1866 workers pushed sixty-five miles of new iron track across the West in one month.

Out ahead of the rail crew were the surveyors, working in wilderness hundreds of miles up the proposed route. They had a support crew of transitmen and chainmen who handled the surveying equipment. The surveyors staked out paths through hostile Native American lands.

The boss graders followed the surveyors. Their job was to devise ways to slice off the sides of granite mountains and use the rock to fill the canyon next to it. When holes could not be bored in mountains, these men ramrodded track over or around them.

The boss graders, surveyors, and rust eaters performed some of the hardest tasks imaginable. On nights and weekends, especially after payday, these workers were ready to unwind after a long day's work. And the rolling camps that followed the railroad had a full ensemble of professional freeloaders to help separate the workers from their paychecks.

According to one reporter, the base camps became "hell on wheels," where "a full compliment of saloonkeepers, prostitutes,

Surveyors prepared the way for the men laying the rails. Trains carrying the rails progressed along as crews finished laying the track.

Thousands of Chinese immigrants worked on the Central Pacific. They often performed the most dangerous blasting jobs as track laying proceeded through the Rocky Mountains.

and gamblers of the roughest sort turned the camps into roaring impromptu cities full of gold, lust, and death." [39]

By the close of 1866 the Union Pacific had reached North Platte, Nebraska. By 1867 the road snaked past Cheyenne, Wyoming. The following year, the railroad was near Ogden, Utah.

Chinese Workers on the Central Pacific

Meanwhile, a thousand miles away in California, the Central Pacific was pushing east. The railroad broke ground when a shovelful of earth was turned over in Sacramento on January 8, 1863. The troubles that dogged the Union Pacific were mirrored in the Golden State.

Since most men were busy panning for gold, there was a labor shortage. Someone suggested using Chinese men as laborers. Few on the Central Pacific Company board believed that these men, who averaged about 110 pounds, could build a mountain railroad. But when Irish workers went on strike, fifty Chinese men were hired. Before long, the Central Pacific had emptied San Francisco's Chinatown of able-bodied men. The railroad sought out a labor contractor who brought farmworkers from China's Guangdong province. They accepted passage money loaned by agents (about $40), which they had to repay at high rates of interest when they began work.

The young Asians were formed into small gangs of twelve to twenty men. Each gang had its own cook and headman who acted as interpreter and clerk. The men were eager to learn and worked very hard. They loved to gamble, but were not as interested as their white counterparts in drinking and prostitutes on payday. Bosses complained because they liked to bathe every day, but their fondness for drinking huge quantities of boiled tea kept them in good health. (White workers carelessly quaffed ditch water and were sick all the time.)

Armed with sledgehammers, iron hand-drills, and kegs of black powder, the Chinese workers carved a railroad through solid rock. In the steepest mountains, workers were lowered down the face of cliffs in wicker baskets. Dangling two thousand feet above the ground, the men pounded two-and-a-half-inch-wide holes in the mountain and tamped them full of gunpowder. After setting and lighting fuses, the baskets were pulled up just high enough to be out of the range of the blast.

With their traditional love of fireworks, the Chinese "powder monkeys" learned to set off entire rounds of charges at once. The louder the blast, they believed, the more likely it was to scare off personal devils and imps.

Laying Down the Union Pacific Track

Back in the East, the Union Pacific was laying down track on the flat prairies at a record rate. Some three hundred miles ahead of the tracklayers, roustabouts graded the rail bed with horses, mules, scrapers, and hand dump carts. About twenty miles ahead of the track, "bridge monkeys" erected trestles across rivers and gullies. The timber was cut down in Minnesota, floated down the Mississippi River, and barged up the Missouri and Omaha Rivers. There the timbers were cut to fit by sawyers. Finally they were packed on mules and driven to the site.

Behind the bridge builders came crews with horse-drawn wagons piled high with ties. Finding ties was a constant battle on the treeless High Plains. The only available timber was pulpy cottonwood in river valleys. To make do with such soft wood, men treated them with a solution of zinc chloride.

Racism Against the Chinese Workers

California newspapers did not react kindly to the Chinese who worked on the Central Pacific railroad. The press began talking openly about the "Yellow Peril." When the railroad was finished, many wanted the Chinese sent back home. In Bodie, California, the *Daily Free Press* quoted in Roger McGrath's *Gunfighters, Highwaymen, and Vigilantes* had this to say:

"We reflect the sentiment of a large majority of citizens of this coast when we say we have no desire to see the Chinese ill-used in any way; but they are a curse on the people of the coast, and we do not want them here. They do not and cannot assimilate with Americans, they are a drain upon the interests of the country, as their accumulations are removed from our shores; they deprive our youth and women of the lighter employments, contributing to make hoodlums of the one, and in thousands of instances forcing the other from legitimate occupations; they have engrafted new and heretofore unknown vices upon thousands of people (opium addiction), and if given unlimited freedom on our shores they will in time overrun the entire country."

In 1880 California passed a law that outlawed employment of Chinese people by all corporations.

The work train was called the perpetual train because it never stopped for long. It was pushed by a locomotive, rather than pulled. The lead car contained the tool and black-smith shops. Next came three barnlike sleeping cars, eighty-five feet long, that were lined with bunks stacked three high. Because these were always filled to capacity, men swung hammocks between the bunks. Some even pitched tents on the roofs. About 300 to 400 men were housed this way. Next came the dining car with a single table running its entire length. This operation fed 125 men at once. Dishes were nailed in place and were simply swabbed out with rags between eating shifts.

Finally followed a boxcar divided into three sections—kitchen, storeroom, and engineers' office. Hanging on spiked hooks outside the car were the butchered carcasses of freshly slaughtered cattle.

Building Towns

As the railroad advanced, a town was built every sixty miles along the track. The first building erected would be a saloon, complete with gambling and prostitution. Fast-dollar types followed the Union Pacific camp. A *New York Times* reporter wrote about what he saw:

> These women are expensive articles, and come in for a large share of the money wasted. In broad daylight they may be seen gliding through the dusty streets carrying fancy derringers slung to their waists, with which tools they are dangerously expert. Western chivalry will not allow them to be abused by any man they may have robbed. Mostly everyone seems bent on debauchery and dissipation.[40]

In the West, on the Central Pacific, this type of rolling "hell on wheels" was not tolerated. Since it was pushing through deserted, harsh terrain, it was easier for management to discourage drinking and gambling.

Hard Rain and Horrendous Snow

It was easier for the workers to fight human-made pitfalls than those devised by nature. Shattering storms pounced upon the Union Pacific workers with frightening regularity. William Henry Jackson, a well-known photographer, wrote about a storm on the open prairie.

> It came down raging and howling like a madman. It rocked and shook us. . . . The rain came down in steady torrents—the roaring thunder and the flashing lightning were incessant, reverberating through the heavens with an awful majesty. The rain came right through the wagon sheets so we hauled a buffalo robe over our heads.[41]

If summers were bad, winters were worse. The winter of 1866–1867 was talked about for years by those who lived through it. Union Pacific operations stopped dead on the snow-bound track. But the Missouri River froze so thick that it was possible to lay down temporary feeder rails on the ice. This allowed Union Pacific crews to stockpile material far upriver. The spring thaw, however, ripped away bridges, track, and whole embankments.

The winter of 1866 was even worse for the Central Pacific. It caught the crew at their highest, most exposed, and most vulnerable point in the High Sierras. Six thousand Chinese workers spent the winter boring the Summit Tunnel. The work would have been

European and Asian workers mingle as the last mile of the Central Pacific is laid.

horrendous in the best weather—a twenty-foot-high hole had to be blown through 1,659 feet of solid granite, 7,032 feet above sea level. After that, it was downhill to Nevada.

Then the blizzards came. Then another, then another. Before the winter was over, forty-four blizzards blasted the summit. One storm lasted thirteen days with no letup and dumped ten feet of snow. Twelve locomotives broke down trying to plow through the drifts. Food and blasting powder had to be dragged in by horse-drawn sleds to the isolated tunnelers. When conditions became absolutely impossible, work crews were cut off for weeks at a time. They existed on emergency rations.

Winds from the Pacific blew the snow into high ridges that came crashing down in avalanches. At least twenty workers died in one such snowslide. Cuts and canyons filled with snowdrifts sixty feet deep. The Chinese workers lived and worked *under* the snow. They had to dig tunnels to get to the mountain to chip away at the granite.

Crews labored around the clock, using as many as five hundred kegs of powder a day. Still, progress was measured at eight inches in twenty-four hours. The mountain resisted the handheld iron drills, and holes had to be drilled deep or the powder would simply blast out like a cannon.

When nitroglycerin was brought in, the work proceeded at twice the pace. By the following November, rail was laid in Summit Tunnel. In all, fifteen tunnels were bored through the mountains. After that, the relative flat of the Nevada desert appeared simple by comparison.

Promontory Point

The Central Pacific and the Union Pacific were in a race by the end of 1868. Each railroad company built full speed ahead on the assumption that whoever laid the most rail was going to own the most railroad. The Central Pacific thought its days would be easier once it was in the Nevada desert. But it had not counted on its supply lines in the West blocked with the same type of winter snows that had halted progress the year before. To keep the tracks in the Sierra Nevada clear, men went to work building timber roofs over the most frequently blocked section. Still the work went on. One reporter witnessed half a mile of track laid in a mere twenty-eight minutes.

Coming from the east, the Union Pacific was finally running into the same problems that had dogged the Central Pacific in the mountains. Although it only needed to blast four tunnels through the Wasatch Range in Utah, it still slowed the rail race to a crawl. One tunnel was so hard to clear that the Union Pacific simply built a temporary loop around it.

Now the grading race began in earnest. At last the construction gangs met in the Utah desert. The advancing survey lines, one moving east, the other moving west, met and went right past each other. The crews were so close that one crew would have to dodge the flying sod thrown up by the blasting charges of the other. Neither crew told the other when they were about to blast.

The grading race roused the attention of the federal government. In 1869 the secretary of the interior picked a team of civil engineers to go west and decide where the rail lines would be joined. They chose Promontory Point, fifty-six miles west of Ogden, Utah. The two railroad companies, after threats, intimidation, and backroom intrigue, finally agreed.

Though the race was officially over, workers continued to lay track at a furious pace. On April 28, 1869, Chinese track gangs

Western Rail Riders

The Pacific Railroad brought millions of Easterners in contact with the Western frontier for the first time. For many travelers it was their first contact with Native Americans and the first time they had seen the Rocky Mountains, buffalo, and the desert. The exotic frontier enthralled even those from far-off Europe. In 1876 Polish novelist Henryk Sienkiewicz wrote down his impressions of some men he saw on the train. His descriptions are excerpted from Keith Wheeler's *The Railroaders*.

"They are not elegant, carefully dressed gentlemen, but bearded and mustached individuals dressed in ragged garments, carrying dirty bundles, and with revolvers stuck in their belts. Their talk is loud and stormy and filled with profanity. Clouds of tobacco smoke rise to the ceiling of the coaches. Doors slam as they are opened and closed by strong hands. References to the Sioux and Pawnees, Indian tribes inhabiting Nebraska and the Dakotas, are frequently heard in conversation."

spiked ten miles of track in twelve hours to prove their superiority over the Union Pacific crews.

On May 10, the last pair of rails was laid and a laurel tie was slipped beneath the last joint. The two locomotives from opposite ends of the country met nose to nose—cowcatcher to cowcatcher. Two golden spikes were dropped into drilled holes, along with a silver spike. At the same time the telegraph system was completed. The telegraph operator wired a simple message: "Done." Guns boomed in Sacramento, and San Franciscans danced in the street.

Five days later, the nation's first transcontinental railroad announced the beginning of regular passenger service. The first full year of operation saw 150,000 people taking that journey west. A decade later that number had soared to 1 million. For $100, first-class passengers could ride in luxurious cars with fine plush seats, and sleeping berths at night. For an extra $4 a day they could dine on food that rivaled the best restaurants of the time. Short-haul passengers could pay 8 cents a mile and get on and off at the 230 passenger stations that dotted the route from Omaha to Sacramento.

Railroads Across the West

In 1893 the last spike was driven into the Great Northern Railroad. This was the fifth transcontinental line completed within a thirty-year time span. The railroads now

On May 10, 1869, the Central Pacific and the Union Pacific met at Promontory Point, Utah. Almost immediately after the joining, transcontinental railroad service began.

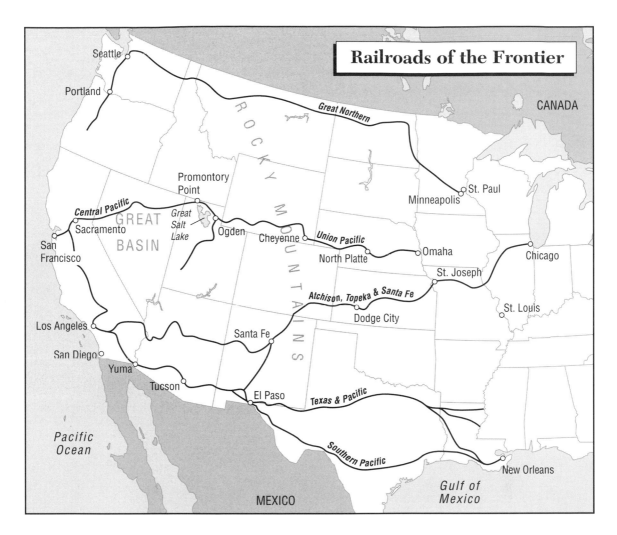

Railroads of the Frontier

connected the country with a spiderweb of main lines, feeder lines, and spurs.

The Atchison, Topeka, and Santa Fe spanned the Southwest and went on to Los Angeles. The Southern Pacific connected Louisiana and Texas with Arizona and California. The Great Northern brought giant timber from the Pacific Northwest to the Midwest and beyond. The heartland of the country was crisscrossed by the Union Pacific. Towns sprang up along the lines almost overnight.

And the railroads filled the lands they crossed with people. The Union Pacific set up expositions and fairs to entice people to move to the Great Plains and California. It went to Europe and recruited Germans, Scandinavians, Russians, and Scots to fill up the farmlands. For eons, these lands had marked time by passing seasons. Now, time was marked by train conductors in tailored coats and brass buttons checking watches that marked hours, minutes, and seconds.

Cowboys and Cattlemen

While huge teams of men were laying track across the Great Plains, the area was not completely empty. It was full of huge ranches, millions of cows, and those hard-working hombres in the saddle—cowboys.

The cowboy is one of the most romantic figures of the Old West. But his popular image does not often square with reality. Real cowboys were poorly paid laborers. They rode endless miles in the snow, wind, and rain. In the summer, the scorching prairie sun beat down on their brains. Most of their time was spent fixing fences and chasing down lost calves. Some men actually did bust broncos, shoot it out with Indians, and lasso bears, but these feats were not common to the life of the average wrangler. Yet tales of rare and reckless deeds helped enshrine the cowboys as the heroes of some of America's boldest legends.

The Cowboy's Spanish Roots

Fifty years before the beef business sprang up out of the prairie grasses, the first cowboys lived in Spanish California. Professional horsemen, called *vaqueros*, developed the equipment, techniques, and language that would later be associated with the American cowboy. When Franciscan monks arrived in California in 1769, they brought with them a few small herds of dairy and beef cattle. The cow thrived in the warm, grassy valleys and became a source of profit to the fathers. At San

Diego and other California ports, the mission cattle were traded to passing ships.

Many of the padres were the sons of Spanish nobility and well-trained horsemen. The mission fathers taught the local Native Americans all they knew about riding and roping cattle.

Many words associated with cowboys grew from Spanish roots. The padres used a

Spanish vaqueros were the first horsemen to roam the western frontier. The tools of their trade were later adopted by the American cowboys.

rope to snare a steer called a *la reata*, which was later Americanized as "lariat." The native horsemen used thick leather pants to protect their legs in the brush called *chaparreras*, later shortened to "chaps." Every year the men would show their skills at the *rodeo*, which means roundup. Even the word *vaquero* was distorted by Americans into "buckaroo."

When Mexico broke away from Spain in 1821, the vaqueros went to work at private rancheros. They boasted a huge salary of $14 a month, which was spent on decorative clothing and saddles trimmed with silver. In 1846, when Mexico and the United States went to war, the rancheros were taken over by Native American and white marauders. Cattle were stolen, driven off, and slaughtered. Drought killed many more. Thirty years later, the men who herded cattle spoke English. But they still swung a lariat, wore chaps, and got congregated with buckaroos to compete in rodeos.

The Age of the Cowboy

The age of the American cowboy lasted barely twenty-five years. After the Civil War, until droughts hit in the mid-1880s, there were about forty thousand cowboys who rode the cattle trails. They were mostly young men—the average age was twenty-four. But mere numbers cannot dim the lasting appeal they generated during their time.

The men who were cowboys represented a huge cross-section of humanity. About one in six was Mexican and a similar proportion was black. (Many black cowboys were freed slaves from Texas ranches where they had been taught the skills of riding and roping.) Other cowboys were full-blooded or part Native American. A number of cowboys were Civil War veterans from the Midwest or the East Coast. Finally, there were rich European adventure-seekers, penniless peasants, drifters, and bums.

Most cowboys were uneducated men who could not make a living in fast-paced cities. As one Texan remarked: "Well, when I got so I could draw a cow and mark a few brands on the slate, I figured I was too smart to stay in school."[42] Other cowboys were running from the law. They had names such as Bronco Jim or Wyomin' Bob. It was easy to escape into cattle country because it was considered impolite to inquire too closely about a man's background.

After the Civil War, cowboys might have been dressed in the ragged remnants of their old army uniforms. In those days cowboys would round up thousands of half-wild longhorns and drive them a thousand miles to market. Thirty years later, cowboys dressed in the standard uniform of Levis, high-heeled, pointy-toed boots, and Stetson hats. Latter-day cowboys would spend days mowing hay fields or breeding prized shorthorns. In winter they might collect firewood or hunt wolves that preyed on cattle.

Cowboy Country

By 1880 people in the East and the Midwest were enjoying gaslit homes, horse-drawn trolley cars, and a factory-driven economy. But the Wild West remained just that. Between California and the Mississippi River there were only six towns with a population that exceeded five thousand. Only a single rail line crossed the "Great American Desert." Here, twenty inches of rain fell annually, and the only trees that grew were cottonwood, hackberry, and a few pines. The soil was mostly clay and sand. When Boston historian Francis Parkman visited the Great Plains, he wrote:

No living thing was moving throughout the vast landscape, except lizards that darted over the sand and through the rank grass and prickly pears. . . . Before and behind us, the level monotony of the plain was unbroken as far as the eye could reach. Sometimes it glared in the sun, an expanse of hot, bare sand. Skulls and whitening bones of buffalo were scattered everywhere.[43]

But Parkman missed the importance of the grasses he so complained about. The grama and buffalo grasses were remarkably nutritious. When 75 million buffalo were slaughtered after the Civil War, the grasses went uneaten for years. When ranchers brought their Texas longhorns to these bountiful plains, the uneaten grasses provided rich nourishment for the cattle.

From April to October 1876, over 321,000 cows were driven north to be shipped from Kansas to the beef-hungry East. By 1887, 5 million head of cattle walked that trail north. And the cows drew men, merchants, and money to a land long regarded as worthless. The chief settlers in this region were the cowboys.

The Cattle Barons

Big business was the reason the cowboy loped across the prairie brandishing his lasso. The Western livestock industry was controlled by a handful of men who owned most of the West's 23 million cows. In fact more than 12 million of the animals were owned by only four men. Together these men controlled over 20 million acres of U.S. soil.

Kansas became the terminal for shipping Texas-raised cattle to the eastern seaboard. The demand for beef was so high that cattle barons bought millions of acres of grassland to range their immense herds.

The Cowboy's Hard Life

Cowboys were men who performed hazardous jobs in a land of sweeping beauty. But nature offered plenty of two-fisted desperation and misery. The harsh realities of life on the range were recorded by some cowboys in their diaries. George Duffield, quoted in *The Cowboys* by William H. Forbis, drove a herd of longhorns from Texas to Iowa in 1866. His diary of distress reads:

"Upset our wagons in River & lost Many of our cooking utencils . . . was on my Horse the whole night & it raining hard. . . . Lost my Knife. . . . There was one of our party Drowned to day (Mr. Carr) & Several narrow escapes & I among [them]. . . . Many Men in trouble. Horses all give out. . . . Awful night . . . not having a bite to eat for 60 hours . . . Tired. . . . Indians very troublesome. . . . Oh! what a night—Thunder Lightning & rain. . . . We Hauled cattle out of the Mud with oxen half the day. . . . Dark days are these to me. Nothing but Bread & Coffee. Hands are all Growling & Swearing—everything wet and cold. . . . My back is Blistered badly. . . . I had a sick headache bad. . . . Flies was worse than I ever saw them . . . weather very *Hot* . . . Indians saucy . . . one man down with Boils. . . . Found a Human skeleton on the Prairie today."

The cattle barons never held six-shooters or branding irons. Instead of watching the dogies all day, they kept their eyes on profit-and-loss statements. Their kingdoms were so large that one cowboy put it this way: "It's as if a farmer in Massachusetts put out a cow to graze and had to find her several months later in Delaware."[44]

Ranches on the Range

While a few cattle barons dwelled in giant mansions, most ranchers worked little family spreads that were the real backbone of the cattle industry. Ranching was a grubby business and most ranchers had little in the way of luxury. Some families lived in covered wagons until a one-room lean-to was built or cut into a hillside. Spiders, rats, snakes, and scorpions lurked in the dust. Poor ranchers slept on mattresses made from feedbags stuffed with "Montana feathers," more commonly known as hay.

Small ranches might have twenty or thirty cattle. Days were filled with grinding work and nights were long and lonely. Cattleman Charles Goodnight's wife once said she adopted three chickens as if they were friends: "They were something I could talk to."[45]

As the ranches grew, signs of prosperity might include a frame house, glass windows, and mechanical rakes and mowing machines. A successful ranch might contain a flowing stream, a corral, a two-story house, a cookshack, a blacksmith shop, and a bunkhouse for the hands.

The big Western ranches were too large to be manned from one central building. Instead they maintained small outposts every eight or ten miles across the sweeping terrain. Line riders patrolled between stations forming kind of a living fence around the ranch's perimeter. Outlying buildings were very primitive. They were typically one-room shacks of sod or logs, or sometimes a mere dugout scratched into the hillside.

Working the Seasons

Winter was the slowest time on the ranch and the only time when there was little work of

Rules of the Ranch

Cowboys were a wild bunch. It was only their loyalty to the ranchers they worked for that kept them in line. But when big ranches fell into the hands of giant absentee owners, stern company rules were enforced. *The Cowboys*, by William H. Forbis, reprinted some rules posted at the 3-million-acre XIT ranch in west Texas.

"No employee of the Company, or any contractor doing work for the Company, is permitted to carry on or about his person or in his saddle bags, any pistol, dirk, dagger, sling shot, [brass] knuckles, bowie knife or any other similar instruments for offense or defense.

Card playing and gambling of every description, whether engaged in by employees, or persons not in the service of the Company is strictly forbidden.

Employees are strictly forbidden the use of vinous, malt, spirituous, or intoxicating liquors, during their time of service with the Company.

Loafers, 'sweaters,' deadbeats, tramps, gamblers, or disreputable persons, must not be entertained at any camp, nor will employees be permitted to give, loan, or sell such persons grain, or provisions of any kind, nor shall such persons be permitted to remain on the Company's land under any pretext whatever.

It is the aim of the owners of this ranch to conduct it on the principle of right and justice to everyone; and for it to be excelled by no other in good behavior, sterling honesty and integrity, and general high character of its employees."

---

any kind. Two-thirds of ranch hands were laid off in November. Many took jobs as blacksmiths or bartenders in towns. Others, called grub-line riders, rode from ranch to ranch and performed odd jobs for food. Grub-line riders were welcomed by owners of outlying ranches for fresh stories and news. Ranchers did not lock their doors, so a hungry rider was welcome to enter any house, feed himself bacon and flour, and bed down.

In winter the chores included the cutting, dragging, and stacking of firewood. The other main task was the grueling business of making sure cattle were not starving or freezing to death. Cows had the mindless habit of standing shivering and hungry in deep snow rather than attempting to find food. Cowboys would bundle up in their buffalo coats and drive the cattle to places where the wind had driven the snow off the grasses. Cowboys also had to chop holes through ice and snow so cows could get water to drink. Often the marooned cattle were crusted with snow, their eyes frozen shut, with icicles hanging from their muzzles. If a cow was dead or dying, the cowboys would harvest their hides.

In the warmer seasons, it was the cowboys' duty to ride the range to keep stray cows on the ranch property. They also had to keep the cows away from bad, alkaline water holes, watch out for cattle rustlers, and hunt wolves, mountain lions, and even eagles, which would kill calves.

The spring and fall roundups were the busiest times for cowboys and ranchers. That was when the horsemen rode out to the range to harvest the cattle. When the grass was turning green, cowboys would brand new calves and gather four-year-old cows to be sold to drovers, who would herd the animals north.

Cowboys spent the summer rounding up animals that were wandering over the huge expanse of wild country. Once the milling, bawling circle of cows was in one place, they could be watched over by two or three men. For the rest of the season, there was rarely a time when cowboys were not out gathering cows. The wife of one ranch manager said the roundup hands went out in April, and did not come back "till the wagon made tracks through four-inch Christmas snow."[46] Range districts as big as Connecticut were considered small enough to be worked by only one hundred cowboys.

The Cowboy's Clothes

A cowboy's clothing was more than a decorative uniform. Every item he wore served a useful purpose. The broad-brimmed hat protected his head, face, and neck from the sun and rain. The pointed-toe boots slipped easily into the stirrups on his saddle—and slipped out quickly. (The most common form of death among cowboys was being dragged by a horse.) High heels helped keep the foot anchored in the stirrups during a rough ride. The tall sides of the boots kept stones out. Spurs on the back of the boots rallied the pony onward.

The bright bandanna cowboys wore around their necks could be used to keep trail dust out of the nose and mouth. In hot weather it could be soaked down and stuffed in the hat to cool the head. In an emergency, the bandanna could be used as a tourniquet.

The cowboy might fortify his pants with a leather seat to protect him from the friction of the saddle. Leather chaps added protection

A cowboy's life was often dull and uneventful, but he was expected to be ready for action if his herd became frightened and stampeded.

against heavy brush, fence posts, and even horse bites. Pant pockets were not convenient when riding, so the cowboy wore a vest to hold tobacco and other items.

In the Southwest, cowboys wore heavy leather jackets to protect them from cactus thorns. In the North, cowboys wore fur-lined, long overcoats for warmth. Buckskin gloves protected their hands from rope burns or blisters. The hat was the cowboy's prized possession. Besides protection, it could be used to carry water or fan a fire. Some cowboys were very conscious of style and image. They might spend two months' wages on a custom-made pair of boots or a fancy hat.

One of the cowboy's most important tools was the rope, or lariat. Expertly thrown, it could snare the horns of a cow, the neck of a horse, or the hooves of either. The lariat allowed a 150-pound man to bring down a 1,000-pound animal. Hitched around the saddle horn, the rope could be used to drag firewood or pull a trapped cow out of mud. If necessary, the rope could be used to issue quick justice in the form of a hangman's noose.

A broad-brimmed hat, a bandana, chaps, and a lariat were common accoutrements of the traditional cowboy. Cowboys traveled light, but each item they carried often served multiple purposes.

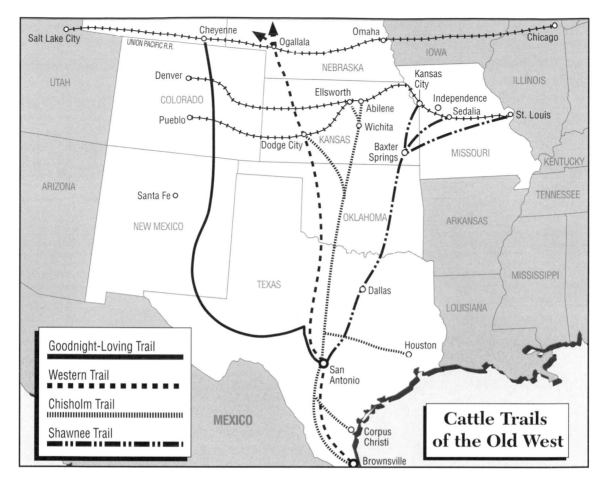

Cattle Trails of the Old West

Legend:
- Goodnight-Loving Trail
- Western Trail
- Chisholm Trail
- Shawnee Trail

Another proud cowboy tool was a gun. Because large firearms such as shotguns were awkward in the saddle, cowboys tended to favor handguns. The favorite was the Colt revolver, which could be used to kill rattlesnakes, finish off a horse that had broken its leg, or—when fired in the air—turn aside a cattle stampede.

The Dusty Old Trail

The trail drive was the longest and most challenging part of a cowboy's life. It involved ten to twelve cowhands and three thousand head of cattle. The trail drive, as one cowboy said, was "an endless grind of worry and anxiety which only a strong physical frame could stand."[47]

There were several main routes that cattlemen followed. At the end of the trail were railroad yards full of trains that would take the cows to slaughterhouses. The trails all led out of Texas. The Western Trail stretched about one thousand miles through Dodge City, Kansas, and into Ogallala, Nebraska. The Shawnee Trail led to Kansas City. The Goodnight-Loving Trail went west to Denver, Colorado, and up into Cheyenne, Wyoming. The Chisholm Trail was the most popular, going to Dodge City and Abilene, Kansas, which was the busiest of all railroad centers.

After spending months in the saddle, cowboys often took their pay and whooped it up in the nearest town.

At the End of the Trail

When the cattle drive was over, the riders crested the final rise and saw the flickering lights of town. The cowboys had probably been in the saddle for four months, usually in the same clothes. Their boots were worn, their hats caked with dust and grime. They had little companionship except for the cows. They had not shaved and their only baths had been in muddy streams fouled by cattle. With the cattle town finally in sight, it was probably neither drink nor female companionship a cowboy desired—it was to be clean again.

But the cattle still had to be watched over. So the cowboy waited until it was his turn to go into town and pay $1.25 for a bath, haircut, and shave. When they got their chance to cut

loose, they did it with a vengeance. "Well-mounted, and full of his favorite beverage," noted the *Annals of Kansas* in 1886, "the cowboys will dash through the principal streets of a town, yelling like Comanches. This they call 'cleaning out a town.'"[48]

On the ranch, the cowhands had to behave, but in town, the rules were tossed aside. Townsfolk were ready to embrace the cowboys and relieve them of their hard-earned money. Starting in spring, false-front buildings were fully stocked with marked-up merchandise waiting for the first herds to arrive.

Down in the stockyards, trains hooted and clanked as reluctant cows were herded into cattle cars. On the main streets, horses raised clouds of dust while boot heels clacked on the wooden sidewalks. Minstrels stood on corners singing cowboy songs, while men gathered in circles betting on cockfights. Prostitutes with names like Squirrel Toothed Alice, Hambone Jane, and Big Nose Kate would lure men into their parlors.

Saloons outnumbered other buildings in town by two to one. Drinks sold for 25 cents. Poker chips rattled and cards shuffled as cowboys bet on poker, faro, and monte. Dance hall girls made the rounds. One reporter wrote in 1877, "Occasionally some dark-eyed virago [loud woman] or brazen-faced blonde will saunter in among the roughs of the gambling houses and saloons, entering with inexplicable zest into the disgusting sport, breathing the immoral atmosphere with gusto."[49]

Outlaws and Troublemakers

Frontier towns were rough and tumble places where cowboys let off steam. But they were also a magnet for gamblers, swindlers, and outlaws. They robbed banks, held up trains, stole cattle and horses, and terrorized people.

Most towns had little in the way of organized law enforcement. Often, private citizens took the law into their own hands. Posses were formed to hunt down bandits. Groups called vigilantes held quick trials and passed sentences on those who were caught. This rough justice was seldom accurate. Many innocent men were hanged from telegraph poles as guilty.

In *Vigilante Days and Ways*, published in 1890, author N. P. Langford writes about citizen justice in Montana:

"Under the pretense of Vigilante justice, a few vicious men enforced its summary discipline. Several individuals were hanged who had been detected stealing horses, several for giving utterance to threats of vengeance, and several more on mere suspicion of having committed a crime."

Vigilante groups often dispensed "frontier justice" with the aid of a hangman's rope.

When the Sun Set on the Sage

The cowboy's glory days were short in number. By the late 1880s, it was no longer necessary to drive cows to far-off railroad towns. The railroads came to the range, and the cattle drive became a thing of the past. The trains brought millions of Americans who were determined to farm the rich soil and build homes and settlements. To the farmer, the sound of the rowdy cowboy's spurs sounded like "the rattle of a rattlesnake."[50]

The new settlers raised flocks of sheep for wool. To contain the sheep, the farmers erected barbed-wire fences on the open range.

This set off bitter wars between sheep farmers and cattlemen. By 1890 the era of the cowboy was over. A blizzard in 1886 had killed off over 500,000 cattle. The closing of the open range changed the land forever. Perhaps the words of the cowboy song "I'm Going to Leave Old Texas Now" best describes the change:

> I'm going to leave old Texas now,
> For they've got no use for the
> longhorn cow.
> They've plowed and fenced my
> cattle range
> And the people there are all so strange.[51]

Pioneers and Sodbusters

The areas first tracked by trappers and trailblazers began to attract farmers and families and other pioneers by the 1840s. The Oregon Trail—nothing more than two wagon ruts—was originally blazed in 1841. By the mid-1840s, a trickle of pioneers made that long walk west.

With about $1,000, they outfitted a wagon in Independence, Missouri, for their entire family. Most had no idea of the hardships that lay ahead—the forbidding mountains, the pitiless deserts, and the predatory Native Americans.

The pioneers began their trip on foot. Only the sick, some of the women, and the very young rode inside the wagons. A few rode horses, but most trudged along, coaxing loose herds of milk cows, mules, and extra oxen. For safety, they traveled in large groups of up to fifty wagons. The "prairie schooners" were piled high with flour, beans, bacon, dried fruit, coffee, salt, and vinegar. Others contained the necessary tools of survival—plows, shovels, axes, iron skillets, saws, guns, and powder. The lucky ones were able to bring a few of life's little comforts—rocking chairs, feather beds, quilts, chamber pots, violins, and books.

The wagon trains rolled in the summer heat and humidity when the temperature on the plains could reach a scorching one hundred degrees. The dusty days of endless plodding turned into months as the pioneers followed wandering streambeds west. "Once started on the journey," one pioneer wrote, "the problem was to finish. We didn't think much about the unborn generations who would profit by our venturesomeness. It was simply a desperate undertaking."[52]

After gold was discovered in California in 1849, the trickle of pioneers on the Oregon Trail turned into a flood. In 1845 only 5,000 people walked that trail. In 1850 more than 55,000 passed Fort Laramie, on the eastern edge of modern-day Wyoming. The soldiers in the fort made a careful tally of all that passed. In 1850, a peak year for travel, 7,472 mules, 30,616 oxen, 22,742 horses, 8,998 wagons, and 5,270 cows passed the fort. The caravans continued until 1869, the year the transcontinental railroad was complete. No fewer than 350,000 emigrants plodded along the trail. The wheels of their wagons left gashes in the continent that would still be visible 125 years later.

Why People Became Pioneers

Hard realities drove people to the Oregon Trail. In 1837 the United States suffered its first major financial collapse. New York banks shut their doors, and in the ensuing panic, banks all over the country failed. Farm prices skidded downward, farm surpluses clogged the markets, and farmers could not meet their mortgage payments. Many packed up everything into wagons and headed for free land in the West.

Epidemics of sickness also drove people out of cities and towns. In the East more people died from typhoid, dysentery, tuberculosis, scarlet fever, and malaria than any other cause. The air was thought to be healthier in the wilderness—and it was. Some emigrants, particularly the Mormons, headed west to escape religious persecution.

Slavery and the Civil War drove thousands of people west. Towns, villages, and farms were destroyed in the conflict, and many families had no choice but to pull up stakes and move on. No matter what the cause, the people on the move were all looking for health, wealth, and happiness they believed lay over the horizon.

The Oregon Paradise

The first wave of American pioneers moved into 250,000 square miles of virgin forest that made up Oregon. The unearthly quiet of the Pacific forests was suddenly shattered with the sound of chopping axes, rasping saws, the low of cows, and the creak of plows. Most newcomers headed to the Willamette (pronounced Wil-LAM-ette) Valley. It was a rich, green valley 150 miles long and 40 miles wide cupped between the Cascade Range and the coastal mountains.

The weather was moderate, and the constant winter rains were a blessing for farmers. The valley was full of deer, grizzly bears, wolverines, quail, and grouse. The rivers provided salmon, trout, and sturgeon. One pioneer described it as "the best poor man's country on the globe."[53]

The first thing a newcomer did was find a site for a cabin. Charlotte Cartwright described the task of building a house in 1845: "Weeks of hard labor were required to fell the trees, clear away the brush, and prepare the site. Trees were cut the proper length, one

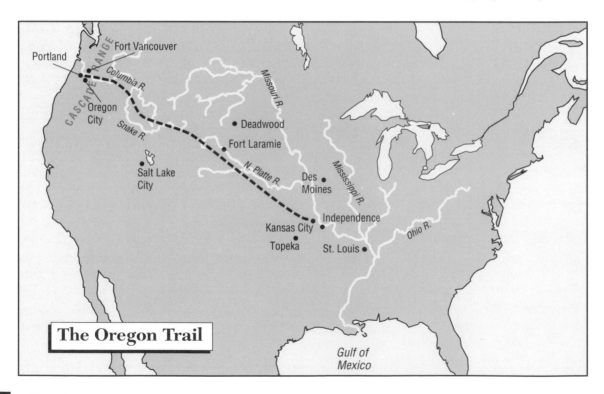

The Oregon Trail

After losing their farms in the East to foreclosure, many families packed up their belongings and moved west in search of free land.

side of the log hewed smooth with a broadax, and fitted so they would join at the corners and lie compact. Logs for the floors were split and smoothed with an adz." When the cabin was finished, "The fireplace and chimney was built with sticks and plastered inside and out with a thick coating of clay. Windows were a sort of sliding door in the wall, without glass."[54] The door consisted of hewn planks hung on wooden hinges.

Life in the Backwoods

After the house was built, the rest of life's needs were taken care of. There were no stores, and almost all items were in short supply. Fort Vancouver and Oregon City were two places pioneers could go to find shoes, cloth, tools, or foodstuffs. But for a backwoods family, that might mean a journey of

thirty miles each way. So the pioneer family was forced to improvise. For beds, pioneers stripped moss from the trees to fill mattresses. No cotton grew in Oregon and there were few sheep for wool. Cloth for garments was costly and scarce. Settlers cut up tents and wagon covers and turned them into coats.

Women provided most household comforts, while men hunted, chopped wood, and plowed the fields. Pioneer women made soap out of animal fat and lye. They extracted dye from tree bark, roots, and leaves. Tea was brewed from sage leaves. Cough syrup was brewed from onions mashed into sugar. When children caught colds, their mothers rubbed their skin with goose grease and turpentine, which, as one frontier teacher recalled, "was all you could smell in the classroom."[55]

Eventually, even the most self-sufficient farmer had to go into town. There he would

Once a family of pioneers settled on a new homestead they immediately began building a shelter. Here, the men of the family erect a log cabin as the women begin necessary domestic chores.

sell surplus wheat or barter it for tools and dry goods. Prices were three to four times higher than in the East. Few settlers had money to pay, so almost everything was bartered. If a family needed metal needles, salt, firearms, dishes, or ammunition, they could trade for it with a buckskin hide. Since a deer hide was worth $1, the term *buck* came into use when people spoke of money.

Before long, Oregon began to acquire the gloss of civilization. By the 1850s, settlers in Oregon numbered 13,000 where there had been 200 ten years earlier. Then in 1851 another 7,000 arrived. In 1852 11,000 pioneers moved to Oregon. The overwhelming majority of these people were men, giving the territory a ratio of ten men to every woman.

Tiny villages grew into bustling towns. Log cabins gave way to neat frame houses with glass windows. Mail began to arrive with some regularity. Portland became a growing town with bookstores, blacksmiths, tanneries, tailor shops, hotels, and white-steepled churches. With the Oregon Territory filling up fast, pioneers were forced to look around for new places to live.

Life on the Great Plains

After the gold rush went bust in California, the Golden State filled up with fruit orchards and dairy farms. The best land in Oregon had long been taken. The plains that settlers had found so bleak and boring when they crossed to the Pacific began to look more appealing by the 1860s. One reason was the Homestead Act of 1862. For a filing fee of $10, any U.S. citizen could claim 160 acres of land. The person only need live on the land for five years. On the vast sweep of the prairies, there was enough room for half a million such farms.

When the transcontinental railroad came through in the late 1860s, railroad companies owned vast tracts of land on either side of the tracks. They began selling farmland for $2.50 an acre. To lure settlers, they churned out reams of propaganda sprinkled liberally with terms like "paradise," "heaven," and "empire." Millions of these pamphlets were circulated throughout Europe, especially in Sweden, Holland, Norway, Denmark, and Germany. They shouted out: "Land for the Landless! Homes for the Homeless!"[56] So many Germans arrived in Kansas and Nebraska in the late 1860s that one tribe of Native Americans learned German, not English, as a second language.

Death Along the Trail

Few people had an idea of the hardships that awaited them on their cross-country journey. In the late 1840s, a cholera epidemic swept across the frontier. Infant cities in the West, crowded with a transient population, were most severely affected. These places had no adequate water supply and primitive sanitation. In 1852 Jane Kellogg wrote about what she saw on her way west (quoted in *Women's Diaries of the Westward Journey*, by Lillian Schlissel).

"There was an epidemic of cholera all along the Platte River. Think it was caused from drinking water from the holes dug by campers. All along the road up the Platte River was a grave yard; most any time of day you could see people burying their dead; some places five or six graves in a row."

In the same book, Maria Parsons Belshaw kept a tally of what she saw along the Oregon Trail in 1853.

"Aug. 25. Passed 1 grave . . . we made 12 miles.

Aug. 26. Passed 3 graves . . . . 1 dead horse. 18 cattle . . . made 13 miles.

Aug. 27. Passed 5 graves . . . 1 horse, 23 cattle . . . made 15 miles.

Aug. 28. Passed 1 grave . . . 17 cattle . . . made 23 miles.

Aug. 29. Passed 5 graves . . . made 15 miles.

Aug. 30. Passed 3 graves . . . 6 dead cattle . . . made 6 miles."

By September 15, after walking 268 miles in three weeks, Belshaw's party had passed 60 graves.

The new immigrants were some of the region's biggest supporters. One Norwegian farmer, astounded by American inventions, wrote back home:

I advise everybody in Norway who lives under unhappy and straitened circumstances to [come to] Minnesota. They have machines for taking up potatoes, machines for milking and churning, for washing cloths, and wringing them dry.[57]

The railroads provided easy passage to the prairies in the 1860s and 1870s. Gone were the days of wagon ruts and dying oxen. Fathers and sons would arrive first, stake a claim, build a house, and send for the rest of the clan.

The Sodbusters

Though the economy of the prairie had improved, the physical makeup of the plains did not. There was no timber for houses nor wood to burn in kitchen stoves. Settlers had to build their homes from chunks of sod cut from the earth with a plow or ax. Dried buffalo dung and dead grass made for cooking and heating fuel. Very little cheer could be brought to such a dwelling. Sod houses were dark, dank, and vermin infested. When the wind blew, dirt fell off the sod roof into the hair and face of the dweller. The sod was too thin in places, forcing pioneers to dig a cave in a hillside and cover the opening with a blanket. "Floors are a luxury seldom seen here," wrote a pioneer. "I noticed yesterday a member of our family making up his bed with a hoe."[58]

The weather on the Great Plains was merciless. The wind blew constantly. Its oppressive buffeting and moaning through the sod houses drove more than one homesteader

mad. Summers were sunbaked and humid. The meager crops of the pioneers were quickly infested with cinch bugs and grasshoppers. Rain would not be seen for months at a time. In winter the temperature could drop to forty degrees below zero. It could become so cold that pioneers moved their livestock into the house simply for the body heat.

Building a House from Grass

In order to build a house on the treeless plains, heavy sod blocks had to be cut from the earth. Huston Horn describes the task in the book *The Pioneers*:

"Some builders staked out the rectangular foundation by moonlight, sighting on the North Star to get the alignment of the walls straight north, south, east, and west. Each block was laid with the grass side down, and the layers of blocks were staggered like brickwork. Two rows were usually placed side by side so the finished walls were as much as 36 inches thick.

In an optimistic effort to keep out the rain, prairie dwellers roofed their houses with a lattice of willow poles, brush, long grass, a layer of clay from the nearest creek bank and a final dressing of sod— grass side up. Even so, heavy spring downpours would cause a roof to leak water like an overloaded sponge. 'Sometimes the water would drip on the stove while I was cooking,' one prairie wife recalled, 'and I would have to keep tight lids on the skillets to prevent the mud from falling into the food. With my dress pinned up, and rubbers on my feet, I waded around until the clouds rolled by. Life is too short to be spent under a sod roof.'"

A photograph of a Nebraska family in front of their sod house. On the treeless plains, sod was a convenient building material but it was less resistant to rain and snow.

Loneliness was the homesteader's greatest enemy. Some people could not take the strain and went back East. One farmer wrote on the door of his deserted cabin: "250 miles to the nearest post office; 100 miles to wood; 20 miles to water; 6 inches to hell. Gone to live with the wife's folks."[59]

Farming the Prairie

The prairie soil was incredibly rich. It had been fertilized for eons by the dung of millions of buffalo. But the buffalo grass of the prairie was stubborn stuff. It sprouted from densely tangled roots that filled the top three inches of soil. Plowing the ground with a cast-iron plow was slow and sometimes impossible. But in the 1860s, a man named John Deere perfected a plow made from tempered iron that could turn the soil efficiently. This advance was also applied to a special plow that could cut sod for building purposes. The plow ripped through the earth with a sound that resembled the tearing of cloth.

Pioneer farming was a family venture. Everyone worked including the father, mother, grandparents, and children. The main crops

A John Deere plow. This invention was useful in tilling the tough soil of the Great Plains.

were wheat, corn, alfalfa, potatoes, barley, and corn. Pioneers also kept chickens, pigs, horses, cows, and sheep. Chores were many, hours were long, and there was little time for rest or play.

Pioneer families grew large. Some had twelve or fifteen children. Women on the prairies filled many roles. They were mothers, wives, cooks, doctors, teachers, and farm laborers. Thousands of women were single or widowed and built their farms alone without the help of a husband or children. Besides working in the fields, women spent long hours cooking, canning, preserving meat, and making clothes—all without electricity or plumbing.

Small children fed the chickens, gathered eggs, and picked wild berries. They also searched the prairie for anything that could be burned—dried corncobs, flower stalks, and dried manure. Older children plowed and planted, pitched hay, hauled water, and tended the animals. Boys and girls of every age helped with laundry and kitchen chores.

The high point of the pioneer's year was the harvest. The entire family worked from sunup to sundown picking the crops before

they rotted in the field. Everyone wore bonnets or hats to protect them from the scorching sun.

Droughts were a constant threat to the sodbusters. Water became scarce as wells and springs dried out. The rich prairie soil would turn to dust. As the prairie grass grew drier and drier, lightning or cooking fires would easily ignite it. Walls of flame jumped from field to field turning the farm families' hard work to ashes.

Periodically hordes of grasshoppers invaded the grasslands. They would eat through entire fields of corn, wheat, and alfalfa in a matter of hours. Families were forced to burn the fields before the insects spread.

The Changing Face of the Prairie

In the late 1870s, life on the prairie began to change dramatically. New farming machines began to make pioneer life more productive than ever before. Before machinery, farmers had to limit the acreage they planted. One family could simply not work large acreages of

The Prairie Schooner

The single most important piece of equipment a pioneer could have was the wagon known as the prairie schooner. A wagon had to be light enough to ease the strain on the oxen or mules that pulled it. But it had to be sturdy enough to hold twenty-five hundred pounds of worldly goods. Most wagons were constructed out of hardwood. Iron was used only to reinforce parts that took the hardest pounding.

A cloth cover partially shielded travelers from dust and rain. In the midsummer heat, the cover could be rolled back. The main part of a prairie schooner was its rectangular box four feet wide and twelve feet long. Dangling at the back of the wagon was a bucket of grease to lubricate the wheels. Four to six oxen were required to pull the wagon, which had to be amphibious. A tar bucket hung from the side of the wagon, and the slats were caulked to stay waterproof during river crossings.

In Lillian Schlissel's *Women's Diaries of the Westward Journey,* Nancy Wilson writes about first seeing the twenty-five wagons that she traveled with.

"Our wagons were big and strong, and had good stout bows, covered with thick, white drilling [cotton fabric] so there was a nice room in each wagon, as everything was clean, fresh and new. Most of the emigrant wagons had the names of the owners, places where they were from, and where they were bound, marked in large letters on the outside of the cover."

The covered wagon lugged a family's belongings out West and it also served as a temporary home along the way.

cropland. Farmers were limited to planting about seven acres of a single crop. Mechanized farming allowed pioneers to harvest up to one hundred acres a day.

Steam-driven tractors pulled huge mechanical plows, reapers, threshers, and combines. The clean air of the prairies gave way to smoke-belching marvels of the machine age.

The new machines allowed farm families more time for leisure. Barn dances and horse racing were popular diversions. In the 1880s, a bicycle craze swept across America. Bicycle races added another spectacle to divert the pioneer's attention.

The Fourth of July was a major event on the prairies. One pioneer woman wrote: "The Fourth of July celebrations were the meeting place of the whole county, where once a year old friends met and new friends were made and new settlers were welcomed to the

Every member of the pioneer household was expected to work. A young boy, at left, helps his father clear the land of trees. At right, a young girl peels potatoes while her mother cooks.

Backwoodsmen wore loose frocks that fell halfway down the thighs called hunting shirts. They were made of coarse linen or loose wool. Buckskin shirts were not desirable because they got wet and clammy. Woodsmen also wore a belt that suspended a hunting knife, tomahawk, bullet pouch, and gunpowder horn. To protect their legs from brush, men wore leather leggings below the knees. Some imitated the dress of Native Americans and wore breechcloths.

Women wore simple linen dresses with a petticoat underneath. Most women thought themselves lucky if they owned a sunbonnet, a handkerchief, or a bed gown. In the summer they went barefoot. In winter, moccasins were footwear for all. This manner of attire shocked Europeans who passed through the area. An Anglican clergyman named Charles Woodsmason tried to give religious instruction to backwoods people in South Carolina in 1768. Woodsmason writes of how women dressed in an excerpt from Paul O'Neil's *The Frontiersmen:*

"[These women are] the lowest Pack of Wretches my Eyes ever saw. As wild as the very Deer. How would the Polite People of London stare to see the Females (many very pretty) come to Service in Shifts and short Petticoat only, barefoot and barelegged. The Young Women have a most uncommon Practice which I cannot break them off. They draw their shift as tight as possible to the Body and pin it close, to shew the roundness of their Breasts and slender Waists."

county."[60] Parades, band concerts, and patriotic speeches filled the day. Families gathered for great picnics and community dances. Everywhere, from morning until night, there were fireworks.

By the end of the 1800s, towns like Topeka, Kansas, and Des Moines, Iowa, had grown into major cities. They boasted such luxuries as electric lights, telephones, trolley cars, and paved streets. The sodbusters now lived in frame homes shipped in on railroad trains. The wild grasses and buffalo of the Great Plains had given way to corn, wheat, oats, and cows.

Farewell to the Fabled Frontier

From the time America was founded, the West was seen as an almost inexhaustible area of new living space. Just beyond the reach of society, the West offered room to stretch, a better life, and good, free, rich earth to anyone daring enough to claim it. In the early nineteenth century, national leaders predicted it would take five hundred years to populate the vast West. But by the census of 1890, the government declared that the frontier no longer existed.

The West had been settled. Railroads and telegraphs dissected the nation. Farms and cities flourished where Native Americans had hunted buffalo only twenty years earlier. The census declared: "At present the unsettled area has been so broken by isolated bodies of settlements that there can hardly be said to be a frontier line."[61]

Modern technology quickly changed the Old West. The last stagecoach rolled out of Deadwood, South Dakota, on December 28,

As the West became increasingly settled, log cabins and sod houses gave way to more permanent dwellings and businesses.

1890. The next day the railroad came through. As early as 1911, ranchers began hunting coyotes and tending cattle from airplanes. Within a few years, cars such as Packards and Model T Fords made rural life less isolated. Far-flung ranchers were able to talk to each other on the telephone. Even the cowboy on his horse was replaced by the noisy, smoky pickup truck.

The American Conservation Movement

This wild expansion came with a stiff environmental cost. Along with the buffalo, thousands of plant and animal species were either wiped out or teetering on the verge of extinction. Forests were falling at an alarming rate leaving barren, muddy hills where thousand-year-old trees once stood. Americans began to discover that there were real limits to the formerly unlimited frontier.

Even in the nineteenth century, there were those who realized that the loss of the West's character would impoverish all Americans. As the century drew to a close, a new movement of conservationists sought to preserve the wilderness as a place for reflection and relaxation. In doing so they kept alive the romance of the frontier—though within the boundaries of a park. The mountains and the forests were believed to hold powers to keep the nation youthful, vigorous, and energetic. When President Theodore Roosevelt's chief forester coined the term *conservation* in 1907, a large portion of the American people were prepared to understand its importance.

One of the earliest applications of conservation in the far West was the creation of national parks. These large-scale wilderness reservations were an American invention. Parks had previously existed—especially in

Artist and writer George Catlin recognized that the frontier was vanishing. He suggested that the federal government attempt to preserve parts of the wilderness and protect the native peoples who still lived there.

Europe—but they were mostly private nature preserves of wealthy landowners. Parks owned by the American people, and left in their primeval condition, were unheard-of at the time.

George Catlin was an artist made famous by his sympathetic paintings of Native Americans and Western scenery. When he witnessed Lakota Indians trading fourteen hundred fresh buffalo tongues for whiskey in 1832, he realized that extinction of both Native Americans and buffalo was eminent. Typical Westerners rejoiced at the prospect. But Catlin wrote: "Nature is worthy of our preservation and protection." Keeping the wilderness was important because "the further we become separated from that pristine wilderness and beauty, the more pleasure does the mind of enlightened man feel in recurring [returning] to those scenes."[62]

Catlin went further. He stated that the natives, the buffalo, and the wilderness might not yield completely to civilization if the federal government would protect them in "a magnificent park." He envisioned a reserve running along the front range of the Rockies from Canada to Mexico. "What a beautiful and thrilling specimen for America to preserve and hold up to the view of her refined citizens and the world, in future ages! A *nation's Park,* containing man and beast, in all the wild[ness] and freshness of their nature's beauty!"[63]

Catlin was not alone. Horace Greeley, influential publisher of the *New York Tribune,* implored Americans "to spare, preserve, and cherish some portion of your primitive forests."[64] Philosopher Henry David Thoreau bemoaned the pioneers' "war with the wilderness."[65] In 1892 the Sierra Club was founded. The first conservation society was dedicated to "exploring, enjoying, and rendering accessible the mountain regions of the Pacific Coast."[66]

This talk of preservation did some good. Arkansas Hot Springs was set aside as the first national reservation in 1832. More important was the federal grant in 1864 that set aside Yosemite Valley as a park "for public use, resort, and recreation."[67] The preserve was only ten square miles and a busy tourist business soon altered the valley's natural character, but the precedent was set. The world's first national park came into being when President Ulysses S. Grant set aside 2 million acres of northwestern Wyoming as Yellowstone National Park.

Although the parks were officially protected, timber thieves and game poachers ran rampant. Railroad and timber companies demanded access to Yellowstone. Moreover, Congress was largely unsympathetic to the idea of a protected wilderness. As one congressman put it: "Why should the demands of prosperity and progress yield to the eccentric demands of a few sportsmen bent on only the protection of a few buffalo?"[68]

The U.S. army, however, went in to police Yellowstone, and it was preserved. The rest of wild America, however, fell to the clearcutting, overgrazing, mining, and farming of a booming civilization. And the battle goes on more than a century later over the last remaining 5 percent of America's original wilderness.

In 1893 historian Frederick Jackson Turner wrote a paper called "The Significance of the Frontier on American History." Turner told Americans:

> To the frontier the American intellect owes its striking characteristics. That coarseness and strength combined with acuteness and inquisitiveness; that practical, inventive turn of mind, quick to find expedients; that masterful grasp of material things, lacking in the artistic but powerful to effect great ends; that restless, nervous energy; that dominant individualism working for good and for evil, and withal that buoyancy and exuberance which comes with freedom—these are the traits of the frontier.[69]

Turner went on to say, the "existence of an area of free land, its continuous recession, and the advance of the American settlement Westward meant a return to primitive conditions on a continually advancing frontier line—a perennial rebirth."[70]

Before Turner, most historians gave little importance to anything west of the eastern seaboard. But Turner was saying that the very essence of the American character was anchored in, and reflected by, the frontier wilderness. So as the United States filled up with motorcars, factories, train tracks, and people, the frontier was seen as the birthplace of the American spirit.

The 1800s in the United States of America saw the most rapid and drastic change of a landscape in human history. The virgin forests, mountains, rivers, and plains were simply *invaded* by teeming hordes of people. In 1800, 5 million souls inhabited the United States. By 1900 that number had grown to 76 million! These people lacked a common heritage that bound other nations together, and they were forced to look elsewhere for the

Yosemite Valley became a park for public enjoyment in 1864. Early attempts at preserving some wilderness areas gained public support, and the national park system was born.

basis of their national existence. They found that common national bond on the frontier.

The Myth and the Reality

As the real West faded into history, the mythical West was born. Books, plays, magazines, and Wild West shows brought to life the deeds of Daniel Boone, Wild Bill Hickok, Calamity Jane, Buffalo Bill, Kit Carson, Annie Oakley, Billy the Kid, and Deadwood Dick.

The early twentieth century would see a West transformed. Most Native Americans were forced into lives of poverty on reservations, selling their crafts or performing sacred dances for tourists. The daily work of cowboys would be transformed into show business at

A poster for Buffalo Bill's Wild West show. Such commercial ventures promised to recreate frontier life for audiences back East. Part circus and part history, these shows were often all Easterners would know of the American frontier.

rodeos and Wild West shows. The discovery of oil in Texas in 1901, along with the spread of the automobile, would set Westerners on a new hunt, this time for "black gold."

The invention of the movie camera recorded the deeds of an earlier time with an exaggerated romanticism. Hollywood movies reshaped the real West into vivid pictures of a way of life that had faded only a few years before. These images have done more than books or history to form the nation's image of the American frontier.

Today the trappings of commercial civilization have replaced the trailblazers and Native Americans of the Old West. Cattle towns and mining camps have become modern cities with skyscrapers and strip malls. Cars whiz across the landscape at seventy miles an hour. Jet airplanes have reduced a six-month walk to a four-hour flight.

For all the changes, there are still pockets of the old frontier among the steel and glass. America's national parks are the envy of the world. The grandeur of the land is, in places, unchanged and unchangeable. And in the long-abandoned ghost towns of America's backwoods, the spirits of the American frontier still haunt the land and the trees.

Notes

Introduction: The Ever-Moving Frontier

1. Quoted in Bil Gilbert, *The Trailblazers*. Alexandria, VA: Time-Life Books, 1973, p. 16.
2. Quoted in Gilbert, *The Trailblazers*, p. 155.

Chapter 1: The Trailblazers

3. Quoted in Paul O'Neil, *The Frontiersmen*. Alexandria, VA: Time-Life Books, 1977, p. 46.
4. Quoted in O'Neil, *The Frontiersmen*, p. 49.
5. Quoted in Bernard DeVoto, ed., *The Journals of Lewis and Clark*. Boston: Houghton Mifflin, 1953, p. xxxvii.
6. Quoted in DeVoto, *The Journals of Lewis and Clark*, pp. 28–29.
7. Quoted in DeVoto, *The Journals of Lewis and Clark*, p. 118.
8. Quoted in DeVoto, *The Journals of Lewis and Clark*, pp. 274, 295.
9. Meriwether Lewis, *The Lewis and Clark Expedition, Vol. 2, 1814 Edition*. New York: J. B. Lippincott, 1961, p. 499.
10. Quoted in DeVoto, *The Journals of Lewis and Clark*, p. 195.
11. Quoted in Gilbert, *The Trailblazers*, p. 26.
12. Quoted in DeVoto, *The Journals of Lewis and Clark*, p. 241.
13. Quoted in DeVoto, *The Journals of Lewis and Clark*, p. 279.
14. Quoted in DeVoto, *The Journals of Lewis and Clark*, p. 476.
15. Quoted in Gilbert, *The Trailblazers*, p. 46.
16. Zenas Leonard, *The Adventures of Zenas Leonard*. Norman: University of Oklahoma Press, 1959, p. 68.
17. Leonard, *The Adventures of Zenas Leonard*, pp. 76–77.
18. Leonard, *The Adventures of Zenas Leonard*, p. 90.
19. Quoted in Gilbert, *The Trailblazers*, p. 217.

Chapter 2: Fur Trappers and Mountain Men

20. Quoted in David Lavender, *The Rockies*. Lincoln: University of Nebraska Press, 1968, p. 68.
21. Quoted in Gilbert, *The Trailblazers*, p. 68.
22. Quoted in Gilbert, *The Trailblazers*, p. 69.

Chapter 3: Native Americans on the Frontier

23. Quoted in O'Neil, *The Frontiersmen*, p. 77.
24. Quoted in O'Neil, *The Frontiersmen*, p. 83.
25. Richard Irving Dodge, *Plains of the Great West*. 1877. Reprint, New York: Archer House, 1959, p. 47.
26. Quoted in O'Neil, *The Frontiersmen*, p. 97.
27. Quoted in Dorothy Levenson, *Homesteaders and Indians*. New York: Franklin Watts, 1971, p. 16.
28. Quoted in Benjamin Capps, *The Great Chiefs*. Alexandria, VA: Time-Life Books, 1975, p. 114.

Chapter 4: Miners and Forty-Niners

29. Quoted in William Webber Johnson, *The Forty-Niners*. Alexandria, VA: Time-Life Books, 1974, p. 29

30. Quoted in Laurence I. Seidman, *The Fools of '49*. New York: Knopf, 1976, p. 6.

31. Quoted in Seidman, *The Fools of '49*, pp. 9, 11.

32. Quoted in Seidman, *The Fools of '49*, p. 123.

33. Quoted in Seidman, *The Fools of '49*, p. 124.

34. Quoted in Seidman, *The Fools of '49*, pp. 133–34.

35. Quoted in Seidman, *The Fools of '49*, p. 143.

36. Quoted in Lillian Schlissel, *Women's Diaries of the Westward Journey*. New York: Schocken Books, 1982, p. 64.

37. Quoted in Schlissel, *Women's Diaries of the Westward Journey*, p. 64.

Chapter 5: Ribbons of Steel

38. Quoted in Keith Wheeler, *The Railroaders*. Alexandria, VA: Time-Life Books, 1973, p. 17.

39. Quoted in Henry Steele Commager, ed., *The West*. New York: Simon & Schuster, 1976, p. 165.

40. Quoted in Wheeler, *The Railroaders*, p. 101.

41. Quoted in Wheeler, *The Railroaders*, p. 101.

Chapter 6: Cowboys and Cattlemen

42. Quoted in William H. Forbis, *The Cowboys*. Alexandria, VA: Time-Life Books, 1973, p. 20.

43. Quoted in Forbis, *The Cowboys*, p. 21.

44. Quoted in Forbis, *The Cowboys*, p. 47.

45. Quoted in Forbis, *The Cowboys*, p. 71.

46. Quoted in Forbis, *The Cowboys*, p. 111.

47. Quoted in Martin W. Sandler, *Cowboys*. New York: HarperCollins, 1994, p. 39.

48. Quoted in Forbis, *The Cowboys*, p. 183.

49. Quoted in Forbis, *The Cowboys*, p. 184.

50. Quoted in Forbis, *The Cowboys*, p. 185.

51. Quoted in Sandler, *Cowboys*, p. 63.

Chapter 7: Pioneers and Sodbusters

52. Quoted in Huston Horn, *The Pioneers*. Alexandria, VA: Time-Life Books, 1974, p. 18.

53. Quoted in Horn, *The Pioneers*, p. 124.

54. Quoted in Horn, *The Pioneers*, p. 127.

55. Quoted in Horn, *The Pioneers*, p. 129.

56. Quoted in Horn, *The Pioneers*, p. 195.

57. Quoted in Horn, *The Pioneers*, p. 195.

58. Quoted in Horn, *The Pioneers*, p. 34.

59. Quoted in Horn, *The Pioneers*, p. 37.

60. Quoted in Martin W. Sandler, *Pioneers*. New York: HarperCollins, 1994, p. 70.

Epilogue: Farewell to the Fabled Frontier

61. Quoted in Paul O'Neil, *The End and the Myth*. Alexandria, VA: Time-Life Books, 1979, p. 19.

62. Quoted in Commager, *The West*, p. 257.

63. Quoted in Commager, *The West*, p. 257.

64. Quoted in Commager, *The West*, p. 257.

65. Quoted in Commager, *The West*, p. 257.

66. Quoted in Commager, *The West*, p. 262.

67. Quoted in Commager, *The West*, p. 258.

68. Quoted in Commager, *The West*, p. 260.

69. Quoted in O'Neil, *The End and the Myth*, p. 23.

70. Quoted in Commager, *The West*, p. 274.

For Further Reading

Roger Barr, *The American Frontier*. San Diego, CA: Lucent Books, 1996. The history of the American frontier filled with dozens of quotes, maps, and illustrations.

Benjamin Capps, *The Great Chiefs*. Alexandria, VA: Time-Life Books, 1975. A big, colorful book rich in details concerning Native Americans and their culture during the nineteenth century.

Thomas Clark, *The Rampaging Frontier*. Bloomington: Indiana University Press, 1939. Hilarious book about frontier manners, humor, and tall tales that gives an insider's view of the colorful and sometimes crazy people who first settled the Appalachian region.

David Colber, ed., *Eyewitness to America*. New York: Pantheon Books, 1997. Five hundred years of American history in the words of those who saw it happen. Includes words written by the Founding Fathers, Lewis and Clark, and less-famous people who witnessed the building of America.

Bernard DeVoto, ed., *The Journals of Lewis and Clark*. Boston: Houghton Mifflin, 1953. The writings of Meriwether Lewis and William Clark, with marvelous details about their eight-thousand-mile trek across the Western American wilderness.

William H. Forbis, *The Cowboys*. Alexandria, VA: Time-Life Books, 1973. A great read for anyone interested in cowboys who wants to know greater detail about their real lives.

Bil Gilbert, *The Trailblazers*. Alexandria, VA: Time-Life Books, 1973. Full of enjoyable stories, colorful maps, and photographs concerning Lewis and Clark, trailblazers, mountain men, and fur trappers.

Stan Hoig, *The Humor of the American Cowboy*. Caldwell, ID: Caxton Printers, 1958. A funny book full of cowboy dialect, manners, and humor.

Huston Horn, *The Pioneers*. Alexandria, VA: Time-Life Books, 1974. A large book full of fun and informative facts about the pioneer days in America.

David Horowitz, *The First Frontier*. New York: Simon & Schuster, 1978. The tragic story of the Native Americans of the East Coast, deals with the treatment of natives at the hands of the Pilgrims, the Puritans, and the Founding Fathers. With source quotes and documents, *The First Frontier* gives an in-depth look at Native American history in relation to the first Thanksgiving, the Plymouth Plantation, the French and Indian War, and the American Revolution.

William Webber Johnson, *The Forty-Niners*. Alexandria, VA: Time-Life Books, 1974. A Time-Life book about the gold rush of 1849.

Stuart Kallen, *A Nation United*. Minneapolis: Abdo & Daughters, 1990. A book detailing a simple history of nineteenth-century America, including Native American re pression.

Zenas Leonard, *The Adventures of Zenas Leonard*. Norman: University of Oklahoma Press, 1959. The journal of a fur trapper who was one of the first white men to gaze upon Yosemite Valley. Written in plain English, this is a great book for anyone who wants real insight into the trials and tribulations of nineteenth-century wilderness living.

Megan McClard and George Ypsilantis, *Hiawatha and the Iroquois League*. Englewood

Cliffs, NJ: Silver Burdett Press, 1989. A book written for young adults about Hiawatha and how he helped create the government of the Iroquois league. The last chapter argues convincingly that the U.S. Constitution took its inspiration from the Iroquois form of government.

Paul O'Neil, *The End and the Myth*. Alexandria, VA: Time-Life Books, 1979. A big, fun book about the frontier after 1900. Full of old photographs of wild west shows, Oklahoma oil fields, cowboys in Model-T Fords, and other post-frontier memorabilia.

————, *The Frontiersmen*. Alexandria, VA: Time-Life Books, 1977. A beautifully illustrated book full of interesting personal stories and frontier history. Includes maps, paintings, woodcuttings, and other artwork.

Martin W. Sandler, *Cowboys*. New York: HarperCollins, 1994. A book written for young adults and published by the Library of Congress chock-full of restored stunning photographs and stories of the real cowboy days.

————, *Pioneers*. New York: HarperCollins, 1994. Published by the Library of Congress, this book is full of source quotes, color maps, wood carvings, drawings, paintings, and restored photographs of the real pioneer days. It is a book about the common people, not the history of politicians and wars.

Lillian Schlissel, *Black Frontiers*. New York: Simon & Schuster, 1995. A book for young adults loaded with photos and short stories about African Americans living on the frontier, including a history of black rodeo riders, homesteaders, soldiers, and others.

————, *Women's Diaries of the Westward Journey*. New York: Schocken Books, 1982. A great book that gives the female perspective on the joys and hardships of crossing America in the pioneer days. Interesting, insightful, and loaded with source quotes.

Laurence I. Seidman, *The Fools of '49*. New York: Knopf, 1976. A book about the California gold rush written from the journals of those who were there. Hundreds of sad, funny, and informational quotes from miners and forty-niners.

Susan Sinnott, *Chinese Railroad Workers*. New York: Franklin Watts, 1994. A fascinating book for young adults about the history and hardships of the Chinese men who built the Central Pacific Railroad over the High Sierras.

Keith Wheeler, *The Railroaders*. Alexandria, VA: Time-Life Books, 1973. Tells the great story of America's Western railroads along with the politics, perspective, and personalities of those who made it happen. Full of photos, paintings, maps, and other entertaining material.

Works Consulted

Irwin R. Blacker, *The Old West in Fact*. New York: Ivan Obolensky, 1962. The story of the Old West written by well-known journalists and writers who were there. Includes amusing stories of the goldfields written by Mark Twain.

John Anthony Caruso, *The Appalachian Frontier*. New York: Bobbs-Merrill, 1959. A detailed history of the Appalachian frontier.

Henry Steele Commager, ed., *The West*. New York: Simon & Schuster, 1976. A large book that details the booms and busts of Western American history.

Alistair Cooke, *Alistair Cooke's America*. New York: Knopf, 1973. A very well written, detailed look at America from the perspective of an Englishman.

David Coyner, *The Lost Trappers*. Albuquerque: University of New Mexico Press, 1970. Interesting scenes and events in the Rocky Mountains circa 1850, with an account of the fur trade carried on around the Missouri, Yellowstone, and Columbia Rivers.

Richard Irving Dodge, *Plains of the Great West*. 1877. Reprint, New York: Archer House, 1959. An informative book written by a nineteenth-century colonel in the U.S. army, but full of racist remarks.

E. W. Gilbert, *The Exploration of Western America 1800–1850*. New York: Cooper Square Publishers, 1966. Scholarly work detailing the geography, flora, fauna, and history of the early-nineteenth-century West.

LeRoy R. Hafen, *Overland Routes to the Gold Fields, 1859*. Glendale, CA: Arthur H. Clark, 1942. Historical records and diaries detailing the long walk through the Great Plains to the Colorado goldfields.

Octavius Thorndike Howe, *The Argonauts of '49*. Cambridge, MA: Harvard University Press, 1923. The trials and tribulations of miners traveling to the California goldfields around Cape Horn and overland.

Nathaniel Pitt Langford, *Vigilante Days and Ways*. New York: Grosset & Dunlap, 1890. An old-time book about mob "justice" in the old days.

David Lavender, *The Rockies*. Lincoln: University of Nebraska Press, 1968. Lavender explores the colorful history of the Rocky Mountain Range focusing on the period that began in 1859 with the first gold strikes. The book traces the stories of beaver hunters, government surveyors, and emigrants bound for the Pacific Coast and includes information about Lewis and Clark, Zebulon Pike, Jim Bridger, and others.

Dorothy Levenson, *Homesteaders and Indians*. New York: Franklin Watts, 1971. A book for young adults about the interactions of homesteaders and Native Americans. Full of tragic stories.

Meriwether Lewis, *The Lewis and Clark Expedition, Vol. 2, 1814 Edition*. New York: J. B. Lippincott, 1961. The original writings of Meriwether Lewis provide three volumes of fascinating and detailed information concerning the Lewis and Clark expedition.

Roger D. McGrath, *Gunfighters, Highwaymen, and Vigilantes*. Berkeley and Los Angeles: University of California Press, 1984. Uses plenty of source quotes to detail the lives of gunfighters, criminals, and other sociopaths in nineteenth-century California.

Lewis Henry Morgan, *The Indian Journals*. Ann Arbor: University of Michigan Press, 1959. Detailed accounts of the lives, appearance, and belief systems of dozens of tribes who lived on the plains.

Parke Rouse Jr., *The Great Wagon Road*. New York: McGraw-Hill, 1973. A book about America's first "highway," the Great Wagon Road that led from Philadelphia south to modern West Virginia. Also includes many source quotes and interesting details about the first pioneers in Appalachia.

Time-Life Books, ed., *The Spanish West*. Alexandria, VA: Time-Life Books, 1976. The history of the Spanish far West with plenty of paintings, maps, and drawings.

Paul Trachtman, *The Gunfighters*. Alexandria, VA: Time-Life Books, 1974. True stories, photos, newspaper clippings, and other information about Jesse James, Wild Bill Hickock, and other gunfighters of the Old West.

Robert Wallace, *The Miners*. Alexandria, VA: Time-Life Books, 1976. This book in the Old West series by Time-Life details the hard work and hard living surrounding hard-rock mining in Colorado, Nevada, Alaska, and elsewhere.

Website

http://www.bigmedicine.com/suquamish/chief.html: This is the Internet site of the Suquamish people that contains the entire 1,600-word speech given by Chief Seattle in 1854. The site also details the culture, history, and modern lives of the Suquamish who were the original inhabitants of Washington State.

Index

Picture Credits

Cover photo: Prints Old & Rare

Archive Photos, 86

Corbis-Bettmann, 19, 85

Dictionary of American Portraits, Dover Publications, Inc., 1967, 11, 16, 18, 91

John Grafton, *The American West in theNineteenth Century,* Dover Publications, Inc., 1992, 28, 37, 52, 54, 61, 73, 74, 76, 77, 82

Library of Congress, 14, 17, 24, 32, 35, 36, 41, 45, 53, 60, 66, 70, 94

National Archives, 39, 81, 87, 90

North Wind Picture Archives, 9, 10, 13, 21, 22, 29, 30, 56, 64, 68, 88 (right)

Prints Old & Rare, 48, 49, 88 (left)

Stock Montage, Inc., 42

Donald M. Witte, *Photo Archive of Famous Places of the World,* Dover Publications, Inc., 1993, 93

Woolaroc Museum, Bartlesville, Oklahoma, 38

About the Author

Stuart A. Kallen is the author of more than 125 nonfiction books for children and young adults. He has written on subjects ranging from dinosaurs to Soviet history to Einstein's theory of relativity. Mr. Kallen lives in San Diego, California, on the bright frontier.

OAKCJ +
978
K

KALLEN, STUART A.
  LIFE ON THE AMERI-
CAN FRONTIER

OAK FOREST BRANCH   OAKCJ   +
1349 W. 43rd ST.   978
HOUSTON, TEXAS 77018   K
PHONE: 688-2251

HOUSTON PUBLIC LIBRARY
OAK FOREST

11/99